TAX Cafe™

Taxcafe.co.uk Tax Guides

How to Avoid Tax on Your Stock Market Profits

By Lee Hadnum LLB ACA CTA

Important Legal Notices:

TAXCafe™
TAX GUIDE - "How to Avoid Tax on Your Stock Market Profits"

Published by:
Taxcafe UK Limited
214 High St
Kirkcaldy KY1 1JT
Tel: (0044) 01592 560081
Email: team@taxcafe.co.uk

First Edition, June 2004
Second Edition, March 2005

ISBN 1 904608 24 8

Disclaimer

1. Please note that this tax guide is intended as general guidance only for individual readers and does NOT constitute accountancy, tax, investment or other professional advice. Taxcafe UK Limited and the author accept no responsibility or liability for loss which may arise from reliance on information contained in this tax guide.

2. Please note that tax legislation, the law and practices by government and regulatory authorities (eg Inland Revenue) are constantly changing and the information contained in this tax guide is only correct as at the date of publication. We therefore recommend that for accountancy, tax, investment or other professional advice, you consult a suitably qualified accountant, tax specialist, independent financial adviser, or other professional adviser. Please also note that your personal circumstances may vary from the general examples given in this tax guide and your professional adviser will be able to give specific advice based on your personal circumstances.

3. This tax guide covers UK taxation only and any references to 'tax' or 'taxation' in this tax guide, unless the contrary is expressly stated, refers to UK taxation only. Please note that references to the 'UK' do not include the Channel Islands or the Isle of Man. Foreign tax implications are beyond the scope of this tax guide.

4. Whilst in an effort to be helpful, this tax guide may refer to general guidance on matters other than UK taxation. Taxcafe UK Limited and the author are not experts in these matters and do not accept any responsibility or liability for loss which may arise from reliance on such information contained in this tax guide.

5. Please note that Taxcafe UK Limited has relied wholly upon the expertise of the author in the preparation of the content of this tax guide. The author is not an employee of Taxcafe UK Limited but has been selected by Taxcafe UK Limited using reasonable care and skill to write the content of this tax guide.

Other Taxcafe.co.uk guides by the same author

Using a Company to Save Tax

Non-Resident & Offshore Tax Planning

Selling a Sole Trader Business

About The Author

Lee Hadnum is a key member of the Taxcafe.co.uk team. Apart from authoring a number of our tax guides, he also provides personalised tax advice through our popular Question & Answer Service, a role he carries out with a great deal of enthusiasm and professionalism.

Lee is a rarity among tax advisers having both legal AND chartered accountancy qualifications. After qualifying as a prize winner in the Institute of Chartered Accountants entrance exams, he went on to become a Chartered Tax Adviser (CTA).

Having worked in Ernst & Young's tax department for a number of years, Lee decided to start his own tax consulting firm, specialising in capital gains tax, inheritance tax and business tax planning.

Whenever he has spare time Lee enjoys DIY, walking and travelling.

Nick Braun, Managing Director, Taxcafe UK Limited

Dedication

This book is dedicated to my wife, Sharon Hadnum, who has been my supporting foundation for many years.

Contents

Introduction

This guide takes an in-depth look at how tax affects stock market traders and investors. The focus throughout is on translating complex tax concepts into plain English and providing advice, wherever possible, on how to cut your tax bill.

The guide contains numerous examples to illustrate every key point. There is also a tremendous amount of unique 'number crunching', which provides fascinating results and will help you pay less tax.

Turning to the individual chapters, in Chapter 1 we summarise all the taxes you face as a stock market investor and pinpoint which ones are the most important.

Chapter 2 illustrates good versus bad tax planning and why trying to save tax should never be your main priority.

The main focus of this guide is capital gains tax because this is the tax that affects investors most... and offers the most scope for constructive tax planning. In Chapter 3 we provide a quick introduction to how capital gains tax is calculated and provide some interesting tables of effective tax rates.

In Chapter 4 we take a more detailed look at each component of the capital gains tax calculation: Proceeds, acquisition cost, the complex share matching rules, what expenditure you can and cannot deduct, indexation relief and taper relief and the annual capital gains tax exemption. We then examine how the final tax bill is calculated.

In the next three chapters we examine some specific cases. In Chapter 5 we explain how unit trust and other fund investors calculate capital gains tax and some of the special tax rules that apply to these investments. Chapter 6 takes a closer look at calculating tax on rights issues, takeovers and privatisations. Chapter 7 shows how gains from options and warrants are taxed.

Once you've calculated your capital gains tax you may have to complete the special CGT pages of the tax return. Chapter 8 explains when and how to do this.

The next 11 chapters cover capital gains tax planning: In Chapter 9 you'll learn how to make the most of your annual exemption by making frequent share disposals; Chapter 10 shows how married couples can split their gains and achieve a drastically reduced tax bill; Chapter 11 looks at how assets can be gifted to children so they can make use of their annual CGT exemptions; Chapter 12 explains what strategies you should follow to make the most of losses; Chapter 13 explains the tax benefits of ISAs and *how* you should use them to obtain the maximum tax relief; Chapter 14 covers spread betting and compares this activity with normal share trading; Chapter 15 looks at why unit trusts are a fantastic tax shelter for investors who have already made use of their annual capital gains tax exemptions; Chapter 16 takes a closer look at taper relief and compares the tax treatment of 'business' and 'non-business' assets; Chapter 17 covers the two main tax shelters available to UK share investors: venture capital trusts and enterprise investment schemes; Chapter 18 takes an in-depth look at the tax benefits of investing in equities compared with property; and finally in Chapter 19 we look at non-resident and offshore tax planning.

In Chapter 20 the focus changes to gilts and corporate bonds and we examine their place in your investment portfolio and *how* you should invest in these important assets to ensure that your after-tax returns are beating inflation.

In Chapter 21 we examine the income tax treatment of dividends and how they compare with income from other investments. We also look at ways married couples can split their income... and all the traps to avoid.

Chapter 22 is all about inheritance tax and how this impacts on stock market investing and the kind of planning you can undertake to minimise the eventual tax bill.

Many share investors ask whether it is better to be taxed as a 'trader' or an 'investor'. Chapter 23 answers this question pretty definitively.

Finally, Chapter 24 weighs up all the tax benefits and drawbacks of setting up your own company to trade in shares.

Throughout the guide we use examples and some of them relate to tax years. Remember the tax year always starts on April 6 and ends the next year on April 5.

We also use a number of abbreviations, the most common ones being CGT (capital gains tax) and IHT (inheritance tax).

You will also notice that we often talk about 'share investors' when in fact we are referring to 'financial asset investors', which doesn't have quite the same ring to it! The latter includes bond investors, unit trust investors etc. There are specific tax rules that relate to these investments and which we highlight but much of the guide applies to all financial assets, not just shares.

Finally, remember there is a difference between what stock market enthusiasts mean by the terms 'share trader' and 'share investor' and what the taxman takes these words to mean. The taxman has a number of guidelines as to what constitutes trading and investment, the latter being subject to capital gains tax, the former being subject to income tax. Even very active buyers and sellers of financial assets are usually 'investors' in the taxman's eyes and subject to capital gains tax. In Chapter 23 all this will be explained.

Chapter 1

What Taxes do Stock Market Investors Pay?

There are a whole variety of taxes that you could end up paying if you are a share trader or investor. The most important ones are:

Income Tax

Individuals pay income tax on any income they receive from shares or other securities.

How much tax you pay depends on how much income you earn during the tax year:

- Interest is taxed at 10%, 20% or 40%.
- Dividends are taxed at 10% or 32.5%, although the 'effective' tax rates will be either 0% or 25%.

In addition, it should be noted that any trading income is subject to income tax.

Although in most cases profits made when selling shares are subject to capital gains tax, if you are classed as a share trader your profits will be taxed as income.

Chapter 23 examines in detail the tax implications of being classified as a share trader.

Capital Gains Tax (CGT)

For most investors this is the most important tax to consider and it is examined in considerable detail throughout this guide.

Capital gains tax is usually payable on any profit you make when you sell an asset. More precisely, tax is payable on the 'chargeable gain', which is the amount left over after you have deducted a variety of reliefs and allowances.

The rate of CGT will depend on how much income you have earned during the tax year, as any chargeable gain will be added to your other income and taxed at your marginal rate of tax. Capital gains are taxed at either 10%, 20% or 40%.

Although capital gains tax is the tax most feared by investors it is also the one that offers the most opportunities for constructive tax planning.

Stamp Duty

Individuals and companies have to pay stamp duty when they buy most shares or other securities.

The rate for shares is fixed at 0.5%.

There's not much you can do to avoid stamp duty (except join the campaign to have it abolished!). However, share investors are much luckier than property investors who often end up paying 3-4% on their investments.

Corporation Tax

A UK resident company pays corporation tax on its worldwide income, profits and gains. It does not pay income tax or capital gains tax.

To calculate a company's tax bill, its total income and capital gains are simply added together and subjected to corporation tax.

The effective rates of corporation tax vary from 0% to 32.75%, depending on the level of the company's profits.

The reason we mention this tax here is that, in Chapter 24, we will be taking a detailed look at the pros and cons of starting your own company to trade shares.

Inheritance Tax (IHT)

Any shares owned at the date of an individual's death will ordinarily be included within the estate for inheritance tax purposes, although there are certain reliefs available.

Where it applies, IHT is charged at 40% on the value of the estate exceeding the nil rate band (currently £275,000 for the 2005/2006 tax year).

There are special provisions for transfers of shares (or other assets) to discretionary trusts or companies in which case an immediate inheritance tax charge can arise, irrespective of the fact that the person making the gift has not yet died.

Companies aren't liable for inheritance tax although in exceptional circumstances certain dealings by companies can result in shareholders paying tax. Inheritance tax is covered in greater detail in Chapter 22.

National Insurance

National insurance would only be relevant if:

- You take on an employee to assist you in your share dealing activities. In this case, class 1 primary and secondary contributions would be payable (by the employee and the employer).
- You are classed as a share trader. In this case class 2 and 4 contributions would be payable by you, as with any self-employed individual.
- You establish a company and decide to pay yourself a salary. In this case class 1 contributions have to be paid.

National insurance is covered in more detail in chapters 23 and 24, where we take a detailed look at share trading and the pros and cons of using a company. For the vast majority of share investors national insurance is not an issue.

Value Added Tax (VAT)

Almost every share investor or trader will end up paying VAT; for example when you pay for software, website subscriptions or other electronic information. For example, if you bought the electronic version of this tax guide from our website you will have paid VAT! However, if you bought the printed edition you will not have paid any VAT because printed books are 'zero-rated'.

In the vast majority of cases there is nothing you can do about VAT. In the unlikely event that you are VAT registered the tax you pay can be recovered in full.

Summary

As a share investor or trader you are likely to pay a wide variety of taxes: income tax, capital gains tax, stamp duty, VAT and inheritance tax.

The most important tax, without doubt, is capital gains tax. In certain circumstances it could absorb a significant portion of your profits. However, as we will see, there is plenty you can do about it.

Chapter 2

Good vs Bad Tax Planning

The primary aim of anyone buying or selling shares or other securities is to make money. This may sound obvious but many assets, such as holiday homes, classic cars, rare stamps and fine art, are often also bought for pleasure.

With shares it's much more cut and dried. Most serious investors enjoy researching what companies to buy and tracking their progress. Ultimately, however, the real buzz comes from making a profit.

Because making money is the only thing that counts and when you consider that, in the worst case scenario, you could be losing 40% of your profits to the taxman, tax planning should always feature high on your agenda.

Take the example of Warren and Gordon. Let's say Warren buys some shares for £1,000 and sells them for £1,500 but ends up paying 40% tax. He will end up with just £1,300.

If Gordon only manages to sell his shares for £1,400 but, through careful planning, ends up paying 20% tax, he will end up with £1,320. Warren may be a better stock picker but Gordon is surely the better investor.

This example is simple and maybe unrealistic but the point is clear. Good tax planning can have a significant effect on your after-tax returns.

Here's a slightly more complex but more realistic example:

David has inherited some money and wants to invest £50,000 in some shares. After doing his research he shortlists two companies:

- Massive plc, his own employer, whose shares are expected to go up by 52% over the next two years.
- Sure Thing plc, a better run competitor, whose shares are expected to go up by 75% over the same time period.

David decides to invest in Massive. Why would he choose the less attractive company? Sure Thing would yield a profit of £22,500 after tax. But Massive would yield a profit of £23,400 due to the favourable capital gains tax treatment of shares in employer companies.

Therefore, even though Massive's share price is not expected to rise as much, it offered the best after-tax return.

The critical point is this:

It's not just big profits you're after but big *after-tax profits.*

While tax planning is a critical part of the process, there is good tax planning and bad tax planning. Saving tax should never be you primary consideration. If it were, everyone would invest solely in venture capital trusts. These are possibly the best tax shelters available but unfortunately they're also incredibly risky.

What's so great about paying zero per cent tax on your profits if you have no profits in the first place? We call this spending £1 to save 40p in tax.

Here are some typical examples of BAD tax planning:

- Using up your annual ISA allowance even though you're not confident shares will do well this year.
- Postponing a sale of shares until the new tax year, only to find the markets plummeting in early April.
- Investing in an AIM-listed company to make use of the generous 75% capital gains tax exemption, only to find that blue chips outperform small companies.

- Selling shares to make use of your annual capital gains tax allowance only to see them soar in value before you've had a chance to reinvest.
- Investing in a venture capital trust to make use of the generous income tax credits, only to find that the shares in the fund fall by more than 40% before you're legally allowed to sell them.
- If you're not domiciled in the UK, investing in US shares because the profits will not be immediately taxed in the UK, only to find that the US market underperforms the UK market.
- Topping up your pension contributions, only to find that you need the cash to pay your children's school fees.
- Becoming a share trader so that you can claim extra tax deductions, only to find that your expenses do not exceed your forfeited annual capital gains tax allowance.
- Reinvesting all your profits after the end of the tax year, even though some may be owing to the taxman.
- And, worst of all, gifting assets to your spouse who later on runs off to Barbados with your stockbroker!

In each case the investor has his eye on saving tax instead of maximising his total after-tax profits.

Throughout this guide our focus will be on realistic tax saving strategies that do not jeopardise the primary objective: to make successful investments!

Chapter 3

Capital Gains Tax: a Brief Snapshot

Although many accountants would have you believe otherwise, the basic capital gains tax calculation is pretty straightforward.

Once you sell shares you have what are called 'disposal proceeds'. Subtracting the purchase cost of the shares you end up with what most investors would describe as their profit.

However, this is not the amount that gets taxed. From your profit you can deduct certain expenses, such as stamp duty and stockbroker's fees.

If you owned the shares before April 1998 you can also deduct indexation relief and if you've held the shares for more than three years you can also deduct taper relief. What's left is described as the chargeable gain.

From this you can deduct your annual capital gains tax exemption. Whatever's left gets added to your other income and taxed at your marginal rate: either 10%, 20% or 40% depending on the size of the gain and how much other income you earn.

A typical capital gains tax calculation is summarised in the table on the next page. If you bought the shares after April 1998 you can ignore the indexation allowance and if you've held the shares for less than three years you can usually ignore taper relief. In these cases the tax calculation is usually extremely simple.

Typical CGT Calculation

Proceeds	X
Less:	
Acquisition cost	(X)
Deductible expenses	(X)
Indexation allowance	(X)
Taper relief	(X)
Chargeable gain	**X**
Less:	
Annual exempton	(X)
Taxable gain	X

Example

Aaron sells shares for £15,000 in December 2005. He bought them for £5,000 in December 2003. His profit is therefore £10,000. From this we subtract deductible expenditure of, say, £75 (representing stamp duty and broker's commission). He does not qualify for indexation relief because the shares were bought after 1998 and he does not qualify for taper relief because the shares have been held for less than three years. He does, however, qualify for the annual CGT exemption of £8,500 and deducting this leaves a taxable gain of £1,425. If he's a basic rate taxpayer this will be taxed at 20%, if he's a higher rate taxpayer this will be taxed at 40%.

Of course, matters aren't always this simple. Every step of the typical CGT calculation outlined above has a variety of 'ifs', 'buts' and 'maybes'. In the next chapter we'll analyse the CGT calculation in more detail before getting stuck into some constructive tax planning from Chapter 9 onwards.

Effective CGT Rates

However, before we go on to examine the capital gains tax calculation in detail it's worth pointing out that CGT is often not as onerous as most investors expect. Thanks to the many reliefs on offer you are likely to end up paying far less than the 40% rate that most investors bandy about, even if you are a higher rate tax payer.

Thanks to taper relief (which protects as much as 75% of your profits from the taxman) and the annual CGT exemption (which protects a further £8,500 per person), your 'effective tax rate' will usually be much lower than 40%.

By 'effective tax rate' we mean the total tax expressed as a percentage of your profits.

You may be a 40% taxpayer but thanks to the various deductions allowed you will only pay 40% on the 'chargeable gain'. The chargeable gain is often much lower than the actual profit.

For example, in the tables on the next page we illustrate some effective tax rates of higher rate taxpayers on different levels of profit. The first table is for married couples (who enjoy two CGT reliefs), the second table is for unmarried investors. These figures are calculated after taking account of the annual CGT exemptions and non-business asset taper relief.

The tables make fascinating reading because they show that even if you are a higher rate taxpayer and earn tens of thousands of pounds in investment profit, you may end up paying as little as 0-25% tax, without resorting to any fancy tax planning.

Even if you earn profits of £200,000 you could end up paying no more than 20% tax!

Remember the tables are for 40% taxpayers. If these investors were able to sell their shares in years of low income or transfer a greater proportion to a low income spouse the tax savings would be even greater.

Some of the chargeable gain would be taxed at just 20% or even 10%.

EFFECTIVE CGT RATES

Married Couples

Profits	1 yr	3 yrs	5yrs	7yrs	10yrs
£10,000	0	0	0	0	0
£20,000	6	4	0	0	0
£30,000	17	15	11	7	1
£40,000	23	21	17	13	7
£50,000	26	24	20	16	10
£60,000	29	27	23	19	13
£70,000	30	28	24	20	14
£80,000	32	30	26	22	16
£90,000	32	30	26	22	16
£100,000	33	31	27	23	17
£120,000	34	32	28	24	18
£150,000	35	33	29	25	19
£200,000	37	35	31	27	21

Unmarried Investors

Profits	1 yr	3 yrs	5yrs	7yrs	10yrs
£10,000	6	4	0	0	0
£20,000	23	21	17	13	7
£30,000	29	27	23	19	13
£40,000	32	30	26	22	16
£50,000	33	31	27	23	17
£60,000	34	32	28	24	18
£70,000	35	33	29	25	19
£80,000	36	34	30	26	20
£90,000	36	34	30	26	20
£100,000	37	35	31	27	21
£120,000	37	35	31	27	21
£150,000	38	36	32	28	22
£200,000	38	36	32	28	22

What Assets are Subject to CGT?

It's also important to point out that not all assets fall into the capital gains tax net.

The table below lists some of the more popular types of investment, along with their capital gains tax treatment.

	Subject to CGT?
UK shares	Yes
Overseas shares	Yes
Unit trusts	Yes
Venture capital trusts	No
Hedge funds	No
Gilts	No
Corporate bonds	Usually No
Warrants/options	Yes
Futures	Yes
Gold coins	Yes
Spread betting	No

Venture capital trust profits and spread betting profits are completely tax free, as are capital gains from gilts and most corporate bonds. Hedge fund profits are usually subject to income tax.

We'll analyze the special tax rules applying to some of these investments later in the guide.

And of course certain 'investment wrappers' (to use that horrible term) protect most of the above assets from capital gains tax. The best known one is the ISA which is examined in detail in Chapter 13 and also in chapters 18 and 20.

Who Pays Capital Gains Tax?

Most investors are subject to capital gains tax when they sell shares or other assets. However, if the taxman classes you as a trader you will instead pay income tax on your profits. The pros and cons of being classed as a share trader are examined in Chapter 23.

You also have to be UK resident and UK 'ordinarily resident' to pay UK capital gains tax. We'll take a close look at non-resident tax planning issues in Chapter 19.

Share trader status is not easy to acquire (and often not very desirable!) and becoming non-resident does not appeal to the vast majority of investors (especially if it's done for tax reasons only!) so the vast majority of those buying and selling shares will pay capital gains tax on their investment profits.

This is why we focus so much of our attention on CGT in this guide.

Chapter 4

Capital Gains Tax: Detailed Calculations

In this chapter we take a detailed look at each component of the capital gains tax calculation:

- Disposal proceeds
- Acquisition cost, including the complex share matching rules.
- Tax deductible expenses
- Indexation relief
- Taper relief
- The annual CGT allowance

We'll then explain how the final tax bill is calculated and how to complete the capital gains tax pages of your tax return. After that we'll take a brief look at some CGT 'special cases': unit trust and OEIC profits, options and warrants and rights issues and takeovers.

What are Your Proceeds?

In the vast majority of cases the disposal proceeds are simply the cash received when the shares or other assets are sold.

However, if you sell your shares to a 'connected person' for less than they're worth or if the transaction is not at 'arm's length', the disposal proceeds will be the true market value of the shares, rather than the payment you receive (which may be significantly less).

Connected persons include:

- Your spouse
- Your children or remoter descendants

- Your parents or remoter ancestors
- Your brothers and sisters and their spouses
- Your spouse's relatives, eg brothers, sisters or parents.
- Business partners

Although your husband or wife is a connected person, it's critical to point out that there is no capital gains tax payable if you transfer assets to your spouse (more about this in Chapter 10).

Example

Johnny decides to give his shares in No Profit plc to his brother as a birthday present. The quoted price of the shares on the date of the gift is £1.25 per share. The gift will represent a disposal by Johnny and capital gains tax will be payable, based on proceeds of £1.25 per share.

There are other situations where the transaction might not be at arm's length and market value will be substituted for the actual disposal proceeds, for example:

- Transfers between unmarried couples, and
- Sales of shares to employees

In these circumstances the onus of proof that the transaction was not at arm's length rests with the Inland Revenue.

The market value of quoted shares is, of course, easy to determine. When unquoted shares are involved, it is likely that the Inland Revenue's share valuation division will negotiate an acceptable value with you, looking at factors such as the company's financial performance, equivalent price earnings ratios and dividend yields and whether you are a controlling shareholder.

What is Your Acquisition Cost?

If you only bought shares in a company on one occasion, it's easy to identify the acquisiton cost for the capital gains tax calculation: it's simply the amount you paid for the shares.

If you bought the shares prior to 31 March 1982, the so-called MV82 rule comes into play. In these circumstances, the acquisition cost is deemed to be either the actual cost of the shares or their value on 31 March 1982 – whichever produces the lower tax charge. This provision effectively eliminates tax on any profit earned before 31 March 1982.

If you've bought shares in the same company and of the same class on a number of different occasions, the calculation gets more tricky.

In these instances the 'share identification' or 'share matching' rules come into play.

Share Matching Rules

These rules have been designed in large part to prevent investors from making the most of taper relief and the annual capital gains tax exemption. Nevertheless it is still possible to beat the system as we will see in Chapter 9.

If you've bought shares in the same company more than once, you are treated as selling shares in the following order:

- Shares bought on the same day.
- Shares bought in the 30 days following the sale.
- Shares bought after April 5 1998, taking the most recent acquisitons first.
- Shares in the 1985 pool, also known as the section 104 holding.
- Shares in the 1982 pool.
- Shares held on April 6 1965.

The Same Day Rule

Let's say you bought 10,000 shares in a company for £1 each two years ago and they've since doubled in price. You may want to hold on to these shares for many years... but you also don't want to waste your annual CGT exemption. So you realize a profit of £8,500 by selling 8,500 shares for £17,000. You then buy the shares back immediately before the price changes.

Unfortunately the taxman will not let you get away with this. The sale and purchase that took place on the same day will be viewed as a single transaction. In other words, the shares you sold are *not* the ones you purchased two years ago that are showing a big profit. In the taxman's eyes the shares you sold are the ones you bought back on the same day.

There will be little or no capital gain showing on these, so you won't be able to make use of your capital gains tax allowance. You will still be left with 10,000 shares with a base cost of £1 and a 100% profit on which you will have to pay tax when sold.

The 30 Day Rule

Instead of buying the shares back on the same day, you wait a week. That's not good enough either. From the taxman's standpoint the shares you sold are the ones you bought seven days later, again with possibly little or no capital gain to offset against your annual CGT allowance. This rule applies if you buy the same shares at any time within 30 days.

The 30 day rule works on the 'First In First Out' (FIFO) basis. To illustrate what this means, let's say you buy and sell shares in the same company on the following dates:

- 1 June Buy 1,000 shares for £20,000
- 10 June Sell 1,000 shares for £24,000
- 20 June Buy 1,000 shares for £24,000
- 25 June Sell 1,000 shares for £30,000
- 28 June Buy 1,000 shares for £30,000

The disposal on June 10 will be matched with the first purchase in the *next* 30 days. The first purchase was on June 20. In other words, the proceeds for the CGT calculation will be £24,000 and the acquisiton cost will be £24,000 resulting in no taxable gain.

Similarly, the disposal on June 25 will be matched with the purchase on June 28, resulting in no taxable gain.

This may sound like a good thing because no tax is payable. However, the investor is still left with 1,000 shares which originally cost £20,000 and are now worth £30,000.

When these are sold there could be a tax charge unless they are disposed of gradually to take advantage of the annual CGT exemption.

Other Shares Bought Since April 5 1998: The LIFO Rule

This rule applies to all other shares bought on and after April 6 1998. Let's say you bought 10,000 shares for £1 each on April 5 2000 and a further 10,000 at the same price on April 6 2004. It's now April 5 2006, the shares have risen to £3 so you decide to take some profits and sell half your holding. Which shares have you sold? The ones bought in 2000 or the one bought in 2004?

This is extremely important from a tax-planning perspective. You've just realised a £20,000 profit so your annual CGT allowance will not be sufficent to eradicate your tax charge. The shares bought in 2000 WILL qualify for taper relief at a minimum of 20% because they've been held for six years, the shares bought in 2004 do not qualify for any taper relief.

Unfortunately the taxman uses the 'Last In First Out' (LIFO) basis, which means it's your newest acquisitions which are sold first, ie the ones which qualify for the least taper relief.

Example

Chloe buys shares in Rich plc on the following dates:

	Number	***Cost £***
• *6 May 1999*	*2,000*	*2,000*
• *28 March 2004*	*2,000*	*3,000*
• *15 November 2005*	*2,000*	*3,500*
• *6 December 2005*	*2,000*	*4,000*

In total she bought 8,000 shares for £12,500. On December 6 2005 she sells 7,000 shares for £17,500 (she also bought 2,000 shares on December 6 but late in the afternoon, after another major price rise, she decides to drastically reduce her holding). Here's how the shares sold are matched with shares purchased to determine cost for the capital gains tax calculation:

• *Same day (6 December purchase)*	*2,000 shares*
• *LIFO (15 November purchase)*	*2,000 shares*
• *LIFO (28 March purchase)*	*2,000 shares*
• *LIFO (6 May 1999 purchase)*	*1,000 shares*

The acquisition cost used in the CGT calculation will be:

• *Same day (6 December purchase)*	*£4,000*
• *LIFO (15 November purchase)*	*£3,500*
• *LIFO (28 March purchase)*	*£3,000*
• *LIFO (6 May 1999 purchase)*	*£1,000*

The total acquisition cost for the CGT calculation is £11,500.

What about shares purchased before April 6 1998? Here calculating the acquisition cost gets a bit more complex if there were multiple purchases prior to that date.

The '1985 Pool' or 'Section 104 Holding'

Shares of the same type bought between April 6 1982 and April 5 1998 are pooled for tax purposes and the average cost of the shares is treated as the purchase price.

This is what's known as the '1985 pool' or, even more snappily, as the 'section 104 holding'.

The total value of the pool is simply the total cost of the holdings plus indexation from the dates of purchase until April 5 1998.

The value of the pool is adjusted each time you sell some shares.

The steps you have to take to work out the gain when you sell shares in the pool is best illustrated by means of an example.

Example

Kirsty bought and sold shares in Marks plc on the following dates:

	Number	***Cost £***
• *6 June 1990*	*1,000*	*12,000*
• *6 August 1995*	*2,600*	*6,000*

The first step is to calculate indexation from the date of acquisition until April 1998 as follows:

6 June 1990 Shares

The Retail Prices Index rose by 28.3% between June 1990 and April 1998. Multiplying by the cost of the shares, £12,000, you get the indexation relief:

28.3% x £12,000 = £3,396

6 August 1995 Shares

The Retail Prices Index rose by 8.5% between August 1995 and April 1998. Multiplying by the cost of the shares, £6,000, you get the indexation relief:

8.5% x £6,000 = £510

The £3,396 and £510 are added to the £18,000 cost of the shares to obtain the 1985 pool (it's called the 1985 pool because it also applies to earlier acquisitions).

The total value of the 1985 pool is £21,906.

Now let's say Kirsty sells 5,000 of her 7,400 shares to pay for her daughter's wedding. The cost of these shares (known as the 'indexed cost') used in the capital gains tax calculation is:

5,000/7,400 x £21,906 = £14,801

The '1982 Pool'

Shares bought between April 7 1965 and April 5 1982 are kept in a separate pool, called the '1982 holding'. Again, the cost of the shares in the pool is added together and each share is treated as if acquired at the same average cost.

Finally shares held at April 6 1965 are treated as separate acquisitions and not pooled.

Summary

Remember you only have to worry about the share matching rules if you make multiple purchases in the same company. These rules will then need to be applied to identify which acquisition costs are to be used.

If you acquired shares in a particular company in one go, these rules will not apply and you will simply use the one acquisition cost when calculating the gain. Even the same-day and next 30-day rules aren't so bad to apply. It's really the 1985 pool that gets messy, and you may wish to get help from an accountant in preparing the calculations.

Indexation Relief

The Indexation allowance is designed to give a measure of relief for the effects of inflation. Here are the main points you need to know:

- It applies to shares bought between March 1982 and April 1998.
- It only applies to pre-April 1998 purchases. After April 1998, taper relief kicks in.
- The amount of relief you get depends on the increase in the Retail Prices Index between the purchase date and April 1998.
- The percentage rise in the RPI is multiplied by the cost of the shares – the resulting number is your indexation allowance.
- Indexation relief can be used to reduce or eliminate a capital gain to zero. It cannot be used to create a loss.

Example

Pablo bought shares for £10,000 in July 1990. He sells them for £20,000 in June 2005. The amount of Indexation Relief he gets depends on how much the Retail Prices Index (RPI) rose between July 1990 and April 1998.

The RPI in July 1990 was 126.8 and the RPI in April 1998 was 162.6. Therefore the index rose by 28.2%. Pablo's indexation relief is £2,820:

£10,000 x 28.2% = £2,820

In other words his taxable gain is reduced by £2,820. The gain remaining after indexation relief has been deducted is usually referred to as the 'indexed gain' by accountants.

A list of indexation percentages covering all investment time periods is contained in Appendix B.

Deductible Expenses

Once you've subtracted the acquisition cost from the disposal proceeds, you can claim costs directly related to the acquisiton and disposal of the shares.

By and large, the only costs you can claim are:

- Stamp duty
- Stockbroker's dealing costs

You can also claim fees in connection with valuing shares, although this would only be of use to investors in unquoted companies.

Be warned that Inland Revenue is likely to contest any attempt to claim any extra expenses. For example you cannot claim a deduction with respect to:

- Subscriptions to periodicals or websites
- Investment software
- Stockbroker's advisory fees
- Tax adviser's fees

Share traders, on the other hand, can claim an enormous number of expenses. We take a closer look at share trading in Chapter 23.

Taper Relief

In 1998 the Government made a fundamental change to the capital gains tax system. The indexation allowance, designed to protect investors from the ravages of inflation, was replaced by something called 'Taper Relief'. The good news is that many investors can use taper relief to shelter as much as 40%, and in some cases 75%, of their capital gains from the taxman. The bad news is that, thanks to taper relief's rather clumsy structure, many short-term investors will be able to claim little or nothing and will find themselves paying tax on profits that are purely inflationary.

Of course, we are lucky to live in a country with an extremely low inflation rate and a central bank committed to preserving the purchasing power of the Pound. The UK inflation rate has fallen from highs of over 25% in the mid 1970s to just 2-3% today. Although very few economic predictions are reliable, it's pretty safe to say that UK price rises will remain low for many years to come. However, even in a low inflation environment, if the tax system doesn't offer adequate protection, gradual price rises can have a serious effect on your income and wealth.

For example, say you invest £10,000 in shares for 20 years, earning a return of 7.5% per year. You will end up with a profit of £32,479. However, not all of this is real profit. If inflation is running at 3% per year then about £14,496 is just inflationary profit – in other words, it does not represent a real increase in your wealth. To have to pay tax on these 'imaginary' profits would be unfair.

Indexation relief used to do a good job of protecting investors in these circumstances. Taper relief's effectiveness, however, depends critically on *how long* you hold on to your investments. Because the taper relief for most investors only kicks in after three years, you have no protection until then. In other words, if you sell an asset within three years you will end up paying tax on capital profits that do not really exist.

It's not just short-term investors who lose out. Because the taper relief rate is frozen on assets held for more than 10 years, its benefits start to melt away year by year after a decade of ownership. So very long-term investors may also lose out under the new system.

However, in certain circumstances taper relief provides *more* tax relief than Indexation Relief and capital gains that would have been taxed under the old system now escape tax altogether.

The amount of taper relief you qualify for depends not only on how long you have held an asset but the *nature* of the asset. There are two types of taper relief: non-business asset taper relief (most share investments qualify for this relief) and its more generous cousin, business-asset taper relief (only certain types of shares qualify). We'll focus on business assets first for the simple reason that, if an asset doesn't meet the 'business asset' definition, it automatically qualifies for non-business asset taper relief.

Business Assets

Since 6 April 2000, the following shares are classified as business assets:

- Shares in unquoted trading companies and unquoted holding companies of a trading group.
- Shares quoted on the Alternative Investment Market (AIM).
- Shares in quoted trading companies and quoted holding companies, if the shareholder is an employee of the company or can exercise at least 5% of the voting rights in the company.

For periods *before* 6 April 2000, the following types of shareholding are classified as business assets:

- Shareholdings in companies where the shareholder owns at least 5% of the voting rights and was a full time working director or employee, or

- Shareholdings where the shareholder owns at least 25% of the voting rights.

There are therefore two definitions of business asset, depending on whether the shares were owned prior to April 6 2000. It is possible that certain holdings will be regarded as non-business assets up to 5 April 2000 and business assets thereafter.

Example 1

Jack purchased a 2% shareholding in an unquoted trading company on 7 September 1998. As he did not work for the company from 7 September 1998 until 5 April 2000, the shareholding will be treated as a non-business asset. From 6 April 2000 the shareholding will be regarded as a business asset.

Example 2

Peter was a full time director of ABC Ltd, an unquoted trading company. He held 7% of the share capital and voting rights from the incorporation of the company in June 1995. He disposed of his shares in May 2005. Peter's shareholding will be treated as a business asset from 6 April 1998, the date taper relief was introduced.

Business Asset Taper Relief Rates

So how much is Business Asset Taper Relief worth? For disposals after April 5 2002 the following rates apply:

- For assets held less than 1 year: **Nil**
- For assets held for 1 year but less than 2 years: **50%**
- For assets held for 2 years or more: **75%**

Note that by 'one year' and 'two years' we are not referring to **tax** years. In other words, to qualify for 75% taper relief you only have to hold the asset for more than 24 months – not two complete tax years (which could be significantly more than 24 months).

So how do these rates work in practice? The basic principle is: if you qualify for 50% taper relief then 50% of your profits (after deducting indexation relief and incidental costs) are tax free.

The other 50% is taxed but may be reduced by your annual CGT allowance.

Example

Peter purchased £10,000 of AIM shares on May 1 2003. He sold them at the end of June 2005 for £18,000. His CGT calculation is as follows:

Proceeds	*£18,000*
Less: Cost	*£10,000*
Less: Taper Relief	
75% of £8,000	*£6,000*
Less: Annual CGT Exemption	*£2,000*
Tax Payable	*NIL*

Note that the annual capital gains tax allowance (currently £8,500) can only be used to reduce the taxable gain to zero – not to create a loss.

Non-Business Assets

Any assets not meeting the above 'business asset' definition will be classed as non-business assets and qualify for the following rates of Taper Relief

- For assets held for less than 3 years: **Nil**
- For assets held for 3 years but less than 4 years: **5%**
- For assets held for 4 years but less than 5 years: **10%**
- For assets held for 5 years but less than 6 years: **15%**
- For assets held for 6 years but less than 7 years: **20%**
- For assets held for 7 years but less than 8 years: **25%**
- For assets held for 8 years but less than 9 years: **30%**
- For assets held for 9 years but less than 10 years: **35%**
- For assets held for 10 years or longer: **40%**

Once again please note that 'years' refers to 12-month periods, not tax years. This type of taper relief is much less generous than its business asset cousin. For starters you have to own assets for more than three years just to qualify and it increases very gradually until you have held the asset for 10 years.

There is a special rule for disposals of non-business assets: If the shares were owned on 17 March 1998, an additional one 'bonus year' of ownership is added.

Example 1

Paul bought shares worth £20,000 in a FTSE 100 company on May 1 2003. He sold them at the end of June 2008 for £40,000. We'll also assume that over this period the annual capital gains tax allowance has risen to £10,000. His CGT calculation is as follows:

Proceeds	*£40,000*
Less: Cost	*£20,000*
Less: Taper Relief	
15% of £20,000	*£3,000*
Less: CGT exemption	*£10,000*
Taxable Gain	*£7,000*

Example 2

David has owned shares in Propco Limited, a propery investment company. He acquired the shares on 20 June 1999, and is looking at disposing of the shares in May 2005.

His ownership period for taper relief purposes is from 20 June 1999 until the disposal date in May 2005. He will therefore have five complete years of ownership. As Propco Ltd is not a trading company, it will be classed as a non-business asset which will entitle David to 15% taper relief.

If David were to delay the date of disposal (see below) until after 20 June 2005, he would then have six years of ownership, which would increase the taper relief to 20%.

If in the above example David had acquired the share in Propco on 15 March 1998, he would have owned the shares for seven complete tax years since 5 April 1998, and he would also be entitled to the bonus year, as the shares were a non-business asset owned at 17 March 1998. This would result in taper relief being given at the rate of 30%.

The Annual CGT Exemption

Investors who make full use of the allowance can protect profits of up to £8,500 per year from tax. Furthermore, because the annual exemption is *per person*, if an asset is jointly owned by a husband and wife, two annual exemptions will be available. This gives a couple a total deduction of £17,000 every year. Over a period of 10 years that's worth as much as £68,000 in tax savings!

It is important to note that:

- The annual exemption is either used or lost in a tax year. It is not possible to carry forward all or part of the annual exemption to the following tax year.
- The annual exemption is offset against the *total* gains arising in a tax year, and not against each gain arising on an asset disposal.
- The annual exemption is the last relief deducted when calculating your capital gains tax liability.

In the chapters that follow we will show how maximum use can be made of this important tax break.

The Tax Rate

Once you've subtracted the cost of your shares from the sale proceeds and then deducted all allowable expenses, indexation relief, taper relief and the annual CGT allowance, what's left over gets added to your income and taxed.

Capital gains are taxed at either 10%, 20% or 40%, or maybe a combination of all three, depending on how much other income you earn and the size of the gain. For the 2005/2006 tax year for an individual with no other taxable income the tax rates are as follows:

- On the first £2,090: 10%
- On the next £30,310: 20%
- On the remainder: 40%

Note that these are just the standard tax bands that apply to all income, including salaries, business profits, rental income and interest. The only difference is the tax rate of 20% only applies to capital gains and interest income. For all other income the tax rate is 22%. (See Appendix A for a full list of personal tax rates, allowances and tax bands for the current tax year.)

Note that if you have no other income, your personal allowance of £4,895 can NOT be offset against your taxable capital gains. For example, if your spouse earns no other income but earns a capital gain of £1,000 above the annual exemption, this will be fully taxed at the starting rate of 10%.

Of course most people earn other income as well in which case their gains are added to their other income. Capital gains are always classed as the 'top slice of income', which means they are added after all other income and therefore taxed at the highest possible rate. A higher rate taxpayer will therefore pay capital gains tax at the rate of 40%.

Example

In the 2005/06 tax year, Steven earns a salary of £28,000 and taxable gains of £10,000 from selling shares. His tax calculation is as follows:

Salary	*£28,000*
Less:	
Personal allowance	*£4,895*
	£23,105

<u>Tax on salary</u>

2,090 @ 10%	*£209*
21,015 @ 22%	*£4,623*
Income tax	***£4,832***

Next we calculate Steven's capital gains tax liability. Note that he has used up £21,015 of his £30,310 basic rate tax band which means £9,295 of his capital gains can be taxed at 20%. The balance is taxed at 40%:

<u>Tax on share disposal</u>

£9,295 @ 20%	*£1,859*
£705 @ 40%	*£282*
Total CGT	*£2,141*

Summary

The capital gains tax calculation can be summarised as follows:

- First determine the 'proceeds'. In most cases this will be the cash value of the shares sold. If the sale is to a 'connected' person such as a family member, Inland Revenue will replace the selling price with the market value.

- Next deduct the acquisition cost of the shares. This is easy to calculate if you have only bought the share once – it's simply the price you paid. If you have bought shares in the same company on more than one occasion you have to use the share matching rules.

- Shares sold are matched first with shares bought on the same day. If there are none, you have to match the shares sold with any purchases over the next 30 days on the FIFO basis. If there are none, you match the shares sold with shares bought from April 6 1998 on the LIFO basis. If you bought shares prior to April 6 1998 you have to calculate the 1985 pool which is simply the cost of the shares plus indexation up to April 1998.

- Once you've determined the acquisiton cost of the shares you can deduct a limited amount of expenses: stockbroker's fees and stamp duty being the main allowable costs.

- If you owned the shares prior to April 5 1998 you qualify for indexation relief. Simply multiply the cost of the shares by the indexation factor contained in Appendix B. This amount is then allowed as a deduction. (Note if you made multiple purchases you will already have calculated indexation relief when determining the value of the 1985 pool.)

- If you've owned the shares for more than three years (not tax years) you automatically qualify for taper relief. The taper relief percentage is multiplied by the gain calculated after indexation relief. Business asset rates of taper relief can kick in after only one year's ownership.

Chapter 5

Unit Trusts, OEICs and Investment Trusts

Unit trusts, investment trusts and OEICs are treated in much the same way as other share investments for capital gains tax purposes. In other words, the rules outlined above can be used to calculate your capital gains tax.

There are, however, a number of quirks and capital gains tax calculations can be quite tricky. In this chapter we will explain in plain English how you calculate your capital gains tax if you sell a unit trust, investment trust or OEIC holding.

The Nature of the Asset

The first point to note is that if you invest in a unit trust the *nature* of the underlying assets is ignored. For example, if you think AIM shares have good prospects you can either invest directly or through an investment fund. The advantage of using a fund is that you can benefit from the fund manager's expertise.

However, when you sell your units you will not qualify for business asset taper relief. This is because you no longer own business assets (ie AIM shares). Instead you own units in a unit trust which only qualify for the much lower non-business taper relief rates.

Similarly, if you invest in a gilt fund your capital gains are not exempt from tax, unlike direct investors who pay no CGT when they sell. This is an important point to remember. Unit trusts and other funds offer tremendous benefits but they may result in you qualifying for less tax relief or having profits taxed that would otherwise be exempt.

Accumulation Units vs Income Units

Unit trust investors who want to reinvest their annual income distributions must remember that there is a major difference between the way accumulation and income units are treated for capital gains tax.

Accumulation units generally qualify for more taper relief and therefore less capital gains tax is payable. They're also far easier to handle when completing your annual tax return.

If you hold accumulation units you do not receive income distributions. Instead the income is reinvested automatically, raising the value of your existing units. For taper relief purposes the qualifying holding period starts from the date you first bought them – the notional distributions you receive are ignored for capital gains tax purposes (although you may have to pay higher-rate income tax on them).

In contrast, if you invest in income units and reinvest your income, these are treated as new purchases and the taper relief qualifying holding period runs from the date of each separate purchase.

Example 1

Ali buys 10,000 accumulation units on January 1 2005 for £10,000. There is an annual accumulation payment on December 30 each year:

Date	***Accumulation Payment***
December 30 2005	*£200*
December 30 2006	*£220*
December 30 2007	*£240*
December 30 2008	*£250*
December 30 2009	*£260*
Total	***£1,170***

When Ali comes to sell his units he will still own 10,000 units with a total cost of £10,000 + £1,170 = £11,170.

For taper relief purposes the acquisition date is simply January 1 2005 and the accumulations all enjoy the maximum possible taper relief.

Example 2

Daisy buys 10,000 units in a fund with a dividend reinvestment plan on January 1 2005 for £10,000. There is an annual dividend payment on December 30 each year:

Date	***Dividend***	***Units Purchased***
December 30 2005	*£200*	*181.82*
December 30 2006	*£220*	*183.33*
December 30 2007	*£240*	*184.62*
December 30 2008	*£250*	*178.57*
December 30 2009	*£260*	*173.33*
Total	***£1,170***	***901.67***

When Daisy comes to sell her units she will still own:
10,000 + 901.67 = 10,901.67 with a total cost of £10,000 + £1,170 = £11,170. The new units purchased are treated as new asset purchases for capital gains tax purposes and hence each acquisition will have its own acquisition cost and taper relief period. For example, the units purchased on December 30 2009 will qualify for no taper relief if sold within three years.

Umbrella Funds

If you invest in an umbrella fund which allows you to switch from one fund to another, such switches are treated as disposals and will give rise to capital gains tax.

Monthly Savings Schemes

Many funds offer a monthly saving scheme and this is an attractive way to invest gradually in the stock market. However, it also means you have lots of separate asset purchases which qualify for different amounts of taper relief and could make for complex CGT calculations when you sell your units.

However, if you're just dealing with units purchased since April 6 1998 the CGT calculation is quite simple.

Each month's investment is treated as a separate investment but because taper relief only applies to *whole years,* investments which qualify for the same level of taper relief can be added together.

When you come to sell your units you have to first apply the share matching rules to identify which units have been sold (see Chapter 4 for the details).

The basic rule, remember, is the LIFO rule in terms of which the shares you have sold are the ones you bought most recently.

Once you've identified which units have been sold you have to calculate how long you have held them so that you can claim the right amount of taper relief.

Remember unless you have held the units you have sold for at least three years you will not qualify for any taper relief. Also part years do not count.

Example

Ricky starts investing £500 on the 25th of each month in a unit trust savings scheme in January 2004. We'll assume for simplicity that there are no dividend payments. In December 2006, after three years, he stops contributing.

His investments are summarised in the table on the next page. On March 31 2009 he decides to put a £15,000 deposit on an investment property. So he sells 5,180 units which are now worth £2.90 each.

The first step is to identify which shares have been sold. Using the LIFO method we count up units back from December 2006 until we have the 5,180.

All units bought since September 2005 are therefore treated as having been sold for the tax calculation.

Ricky's Monthly Investments

Month	Price £	Units	Cost
January 2004	1	500	500
February 2004	1.02	490	500
March 2004	1.04	481	500
April 2004	1.06	472	500
May 2004	1.08	463	500
June 2004	1.1	455	500
July 2004	1.12	446	500
August 2004	1.14	439	500
September 2004	1.16	431	500
October 2004	1.18	424	500
November 2004	1.2	417	500
December 2004	1.22	410	500
January 2005	1.24	403	500
February 2005	1.26	397	500
March 2005	1.28	391	500
April 2005	1.3	385	500
May 2005	1.32	379	500
June 2005	1.34	373	500
July 2005	1.36	368	500
August 2005	1.38	362	500
September 2005	1.4	357	500
October 2005	1.42	352	500
November 2005	1.44	347	500
December 2005	1.46	342	500
January 2006	1.48	338	500
February 2006	1.5	333	500
March 2006	1.52	329	500
April 2006	1.54	325	500
May 2006	1.56	321	500
June 2006	1.58	316	500
July 2006	1.6	313	500
August 2006	1.62	309	500
September 2006	1.64	305	500
October 2006	1.66	301	500
November 2006	1.68	298	500
December 2006	1.7	294	500
Total		**13,663**	**18,000**

Next we have to decide how much taper relief the 5,180 units qualify for. We sort them into groups with reference to whole 12-month periods up to March 31 2009 when the sale takes place.

Period	***Units Bought***	***Cost***
1 April 2008 to 31 March 2009	*NIL*	*NIL*
1 April 2007 to 31 March 2008	*NIL*	*NIL*
1 April 2006 to 31 March 2007	*2,781*	*£4,500*
1 April 2005 to 31 March 2006	*2,399*	*£3,500*

We now work out the capital gains on each of these groupings.

1 April 2006 to 31 March 2007

These 2,781 units have been held for less than three years when Ricky sells them so they qualify for no taper relief. The capital gain is therefore:

Proceeds (2,781 x £2.90)	*£8,064.90*
Less Cost	*£4,500*
Gain	*£3,564,90*

1 April 2005 to 31 March 2006

These 2,399 units have been held for more than three years but less than four years and therefore qualify for 5% taper relief. The capital gain is therefore:

Proceeds (2,399 x £2.90)	*£6,957.10*
Less Cost	*£3,500*
Gain	*£3,457.10*
Less taper relief @ 5%	*£172.86*
Chargeable gain	*£3,284.24*

The total chargeable gains are therefore:
£3,564.90 + 3,284.24 = £6,849.14

If Ricky has no other taxable gains this amount will be easily covered by his annual CGT exemption.

Units Bought in Earlier Periods

If you were contributing to a unit trust before indexation relief was abolished you theoretically have to do a separate CGT calculation for every single monthly investment when you sell your units. (Because each monthly investment qualifies for a different indexation allowance.)

Fortunately, the Inland Revenue saw the light and issued a statement of practice which substantially reduces the number of calculations necessary and will make your life a lot simpler. This approach treats all investments made in a year as if they were made in a single month of that year, usually the seventh month. (By 'year' the taxman does not mean calendar years - the year will correspond to the accounting year of the fund in question.)

For example, say you invest £100 on the 7th of each month in a unit trust and the unit trust has an accounting year ending on December 31. Your CGT calculation will be made as if you made a single investment of £1,200 on July 7th (the seventh month of the year).

Using this method only one calculation is needed for the investments of that year, instead of twelve. The simplified method is available to investors who started contributing before 6 April 1998 in a monthly unit trust, investment trust or OEIC. Furthermore, it only applies to accounting years which ended before April 6 1999.

To calculate your gains using this method you must write to your tax office for permission.

Example

Starting in September 1995, Gareth invests £100 a month on the first of each month in unit trust income units. No distributions are reinvested. The unit trust's accounting year starts on July 1 and ends on June 30 the following year. The last investment is made in April 2002 and all the units are sold on May 25 2005. Gareth's purchases are summarised in the table on the next page.

Gareth's Monthly Investments

Month	Price	Units	Month	Price	Units
Sep 1995	38	263.16	Jan 1999	78	128.21
Oct	39	256.41	Feb	79	126.58
Nov	40	250.00	Mar	80	125.00
Dec	41	243.90	Apr	81	123.46
Jan 1996	42	238.10	May	82	121.95
Feb	43	232.56	June	83	120.48
Mar	44	227.27	July	84	119.05
Apr	45	222.22	Aug	85	117.65
May	46	217.39	Sep	86	116.28
June	47	212.77	Oct	87	114.94
July	48	208.33	Nov	88	113.64
Aug	49	204.08	Dec	89	112.36
Sep	50	200.00	Jan 2000	90	111.11
Oct	51	196.08	Feb	91	109.89
Nov	52	192.31	Mar	92	108.70
Dec	53	188.68	Apr	93	107.53
Jan 1997	54	185.19	May	94	106.38
Feb	55	181.82	June	95	105.26
Mar	56	178.57	July	96	104.17
Apr	57	175.44	Aug	97	103.09
May	58	172.41	Sep	98	102.04
June	59	169.49	Oct	99	101.01
July	60	166.67	Nov	100	100.00
Aug	61	163.93	Dec	101	99.01
Sep	62	161.29	Jan 2001	102	98.04
Oct	63	158.73	Feb	103	97.09
Nov	64	156.25	Mar	104	96.15
Dec	65	153.85	Apr	105	95.24
Jan 1998	66	151.52	May	106	94.34
Feb	67	149.25	June	107	93.46
Mar	68	147.06	July	108	92.59
Apr	69	144.93	Aug	109	91.74
May	70	142.86	Sep	110	90.91
June	71	140.85	Oct	111	90.09
July	72	138.89	Nov	112	89.29
Aug	73	136.99	Dec	113	88.50
Sep	74	135.14	Jan 2002	114	87.72
Oct	75	133.33	Feb	115	86.96
Nov	76	131.58	Mar	116	86.21
Dec	77	129.87	Apr	117	85.47

In total 11,420.71 units have been bought for £8,000. We assume the selling price on May 25 2005 is £1.30. He will therefore have disposal proceeds of £14,846.92 with a profit of £6,846.92. How much tax is payable? Firstly we look at the units bought <u>*after*</u> *June 30 1998. This is the last day of the final accounting period which qualifies for the special calculation method.(Remember it only applies to accounting years which ended before April 6 1999.)*

Units bought from June 1 2001 to April 1 2002

These 982.93 units were held for three complete years and qualify for 5% taper relief.

Proceeds (982.93 x £1.30)	*£1277.81*
Less Cost	*£1,100*
Gain	*£177.81*
Tapered Gain (£177.8 x 95%)	*£168.92*

Units bought from June 1 2000 to May 1 2001

These 1,195.44 units were held for four complete years and qualify for 10% taper relief.

Proceeds (1,195.44 x £1.30)	*£1554.07*
Less Cost	*£1,200*
Gain	*£354.07*
Tapered gain (£354.07 x 90%)	*£318.66*

Units bought from June 1 1999 to May 1 2000

These 1,358 units were held for five complete years and qualify for 15% taper relief:

Proceeds (1,358 x £1.30)	*£1765.4*
Less Cost	*£1,200*
Gain	*£565.4*
Tapered gain (£565.4 x 85%)	*£480.59*

Units bought from July 1 1998 to May 1 1999

These 1430.99 units were held for six complete years and qualify for 20% taper relief:

Proceeds (1,430.99 x £1.30)	*£1,860.29*
Less Cost	*£1,100*
Gain	*£760.29*
Tapered gain (£760.29 x 80%)	*£608.23*

This leaves the 6,453.35 units bought prior to July 1998 which qualify for the special CGT calculation method.

This is applied to investments made in the periods ending 30 June 1996, 30 June 1997 and 30 June 1998 (remember it's based on the unit trust's accounting year which ends in June).

The units Gareth bought during the first accounting year which ended on 30 June 1996 are treated as though bought on the date he made his last investment, namely 1 June 1996.

This is because the rule states that if you begin regular saving part way through an accounting year (Gareth started in September 1995, part way through the accounting year), your investments for that year will be treated as having been made when the last investment was made.

For the accounting years which end on June 30 1997 and June 30 1998 the seventh month rule applies.

Therefore Gareth is treated as having bought:

- *2,363.78 units on June 1 1996 for £1,000 (covering purchases between September 1995 and June 1996 inclusive).*

- *2,252.40 units on January 1 1997 for £1,200 (covering purchases between July 1996 and June 1997 inclusive).*

- *1,837.18 units on January 1 1998 for £1,200 (covering purchases between July 1997 and June 1998 inclusive).*

The next step is to calculate the gain on these 6,453.35 units.

As they were all bought before April 6 1998 they are pooled together (see Chapter 4) and qualify for indexation relief to April 1998.

Because all these monthly savings between September 1995 and June 1998 are treated as if bought on either June 1 1996, January 1 1997 or January 1 1998, the relevant indexation factors are 6.3%, 5.3% and 1.9% respectively (see Appendix B for monthly indexation factors). Multiplying by the cost of the units we get the relevant indexation allowances:

June 1 1996	*£1,000 x 6.3%*	=	*£63*
January 1 1997	*£1,200 x 5.3%*	=	*£63.60*
January 1 1998	*£1,200 x 1.9%*	=	*£22.8*
Total indexation			***£149.40***

The next step is to calculate taper relief. Because all these units were acquired before 17 March 1998 they also qualify for an extra bonus year of taper relief (see Chapter 4).

The units were held for seven complete years after April 5 1998 and therefore qualify for eight years of taper relief. This means 30% of the gain is completely tax free. The tax calculation is as follows:

Proceeds (6,453.35 x £1.30)	*£8,389.36*
Less cost	*£3,400*
Unindexed gain	*£4,989.36*
Less indexation	*£149.40*
Indexed gain	*£4,839.96*
Less taper relief @ 30%	*£1,451.99*
Tapered gain	***£3,387.97***

Finally we add up all the gains for the entire investment period.

£168.92+£318.66+£480.59+£608.23+£3,387.97 = £4964.37

This amount can be reduced by the annual CGT allowance... and that's the end of the tax calculation!

Chapter 6

Takeovers, Rights Issues and Privatisations

Takeovers

Let's assume you buy 1,000 shares in Gordon plc for £1 each. The company does well and attracts a takeover bid from Monster plc. Monster plc could either make a cash offer for your shares or offer you shares in Monster plc in exchange.

A cash payment will result in capital gains tax having to be paid. If Monster offers you £10 per share, you will have a gain of £9,000 (before deducting any reliefs).

If Monster offers you shares in its own company in exchange, there are provisions that can apply so that there is deemed to be no taxable gain and the new shares are deemed to have been acquired on the same date as the Gordon plc shares. The new shares are treated as 'standing in the shoes' of the old shares.

There are certain Inland Revenue conditions that must be met but which are not worth examining in any detail here.

Rights Issues

If a shareholder decides to take up a rights issue no taxable gain arises. In many cases, however, shareholders accept cash payments instead. A sale of rights is classed as a part disposal for capital gains tax purposes. The tax calculation is based on the increase in value of a proportion of the original shareholding.

Under normal circumstances, the proceeds will be the amount received for the sale of the rights.

However, the sale of rights is not treated as a disposal if the proceeds are 'small'. 'Small' is not defined in the legislation. However, the Inland Revenue states that it will treat proceeds as small if they are equal to or less than 5 per cent of the value of the underlying shares (at the date of the rights issue), or £3,000, whichever is the greatest of these figures.

When these conditions are met, it is referred to as a small part disposal and in most cases the proceeds are subtracted from the base cost which essentially transfers any gain arising from the sale of the rights to the year in which the shares creating the rights are sold.

The small part disposal rules can therefore defer capital gains tax until a future disposal of the shares, giving a valuable cash flow benefit, as you will already have received cash when you sold your rights.

Calculating the Cost of the Rights

As with any asset, in order to calculate any gain arising, we need to be able to identify the cost of the asset disposed of. The cost of the rights is taken to be a proportion of the base cost of the shares creating the rights. When all the rights are sold, this proportion is given by the following formula:

Base cost × sale proceeds /(current value of original shares + sale proceeds)

When only some of the rights are disposed of, and some are taken up, the denominator (the part in brackets) in the above formula changes to:

(Current value of original shares + value of rights taken up + sale proceeds)

Taper Relief on Disposal of Rights

When rights are sold, the amount of taper relief allowed is determined by the original shares which created the rights, and therefore the taper relief is based on the acquisition date of those shares.

Example

David purchased 40,000 shares in Quickgrow plc in May 2002 at a cost of £2 per share. In June 2005, Quickgrow declares a one for three rights issue at £2.60 per share. David decides to sell his rights for 45p each (a total of £6,000).

The total value of David's original shareholding is £104,000 (£2.60 x 40,000).

The disposal of the rights is not a small part disposal because £6,000 taken as a percentage of £104,000 is 5.8% and therefore exceeds the 5% limit outlined above.

The attributable cost is calculated using the following formula:

Base cost × sale proceeds /(current value of original shares +sale proceeds)

£80,000 x £6,000/(£104,000 + £6,000) = £4,364

The capital gains tax calculation is then as follows:

Proceeds	*£6,000*
Less: Cost	*£4,364*
Gain	*£1,636*
Less: Taper relief @ 5%	*£82*
Gain before CGT allowance	*£1,554*

Note that if the disposal was treated as a small part disposal, the proceeds of £6,000 would simply be deducted from the allowable base cost, to give a new base cost of £74,000, which would eventually result in a higher chargeable gain.

For the majority of small investors, the sale of rights will not result in tax having to be paid due to the effects of the small part disposal rules and the application of the annual CGT exemption.

If you don't think you will have other chargeable gains in the tax year you sell your rights, the small part disposal rules can be 'disapplied' so as to ensure that a chargeable gain arises which will be covered by the annual exemption.

Privatisations

Many issues of shares in newly privatised companies allowed payment by way of instalments.

In normal situations this would create a problem in terms of calculating the applicable indexation allowance because there would be several share acquisitons over a period of time.

However, the Inland Revenue accepts that in the case of privatisations, the person buying the shares is deemed to have incurred the FULL cost from day one.

Note that this will only be an issue for privatisations pre-April 1998, as indexation allowance was replaced by taper relief on this date.

Furthermore, bonus shares were frequently awarded to encourage shareholders to hold on to their shares for a number of years. The shareholder is deemed to acquire these shares at the date of issue at their then market value.

Chapter 7

Options and Warrants

Options are used to speculate on share price movements or hedge portfolios against share price falls. Either way, the profits are normally subject to capital gains tax. The same goes for warrants.

I say 'normally' because it is possible to be classed as a *trader* in options, just as it is possible to be classed as a trader in shares. In these instances your profits will be subject to income tax. (See Chapter 23 for more on the tax treatment of traders.)

In this chapter we'll examine the capital gains tax implications of buying and selling options and warrants as it's these tax rules that will apply most often.

If you're buying and selling options frequently, the normal share matching rules will apply, provided the options are of the same 'class' and 'series' (in other words, provided they have the same expiry date and exercise price).

The main difference between the ordinary CGT rules and the rules which apply to warrants and traded options is that the abandonment of the option is treated as a disposal.

This means that the grantee of the option (that is, the person who buys the option) will obtain an allowable loss for capital gains tax purposes if the option is simply allowed to expire.

If you decide to exercise an option or warrant, its cost is added to the exercise price of the shares to determine the base cost for the CGT calculation.

Example

David buys 5,000 warrants in ABC plc, which give him the right to purchase one share per warrant at a price of £3.00 within the next three years. He pays a premium of 10p per warrant.

If he subsequently exercises the warrants, his total base cost will be £15,500 (the cost of the warrants and the cost of the shares).

David subsequently sells the 5,000 shares for £5.00 each.
The CGT calculation will be as follows:

Proceeds	*£25,000*
Less: Cost	*£15,500*
Gain	*£9,500*

Of course, the actual option or warrant may never be exercised if you sell it for a profit before the expiry date. This would be a simple disposal for CGT purposes and the gain (before CGT reliefs) would be the uplift in value from the price paid to proceeds received.

Taper Relief

If the warrant/option is exercised and the underlying shares are sold later on, the period of ownership for taper relief purposes will be the period from the date of exercising the warrant/option, and NOT from the date the warrant/option was initially purchased.

However, if you sell the warrant/option for a profit before the expiry date, the period of ownership will be from the date of purchase to the date of disposal. Of course, because most options have a short lifespan, you are unlikely to ever qualify for taper relief if you are buying and selling them on a regular basis.

However, some warrants do have long lifespans and may therefore qualify for taper relief. If you hold on to a warrant for, say, five years and then sell it for a profit, you will qualify for 15% taper relief. If instead you exercise the warrant and acquire the underlying shares the accumulated taper relief will be lost and you will have to wait another five years to get it back again. So it's often better from a tax perspective to sell long-term warrants rather than exercise them.

Tax Planning

Options and warrants can be put to a number of uses:

Crystallisation of Losses

Let's assume Bob holds 1,000 shares in Slump plc. He purchased them at a price of £4.40, but the share price has now decreased to £1.40. He is therefore sitting on a capital loss of £3,000 (£4.40 - £1.40 x 1,000).

He has made other share disposals during tax year and has crystallised gains of £11,200.

To avoid paying any tax, it may be desirable for Bob to dispose of the Slump plc shares and offset his loss against his gains, with the remaining gain being reduced by the annual capital gains tax exemption.

However, maybe Bob is reluctant to dispose of his Slump plc shares as he is confident they are going to enjoy a rebound shortly.

What should he do?

He could sell the Slump plc shares, thereby crystallising his loss for tax purposes but take out an option to buy the shares. If the price subsequently rises he will still benefit by holding a position in Slump but will have reduced his CGT liability by utilizing his loss.

Using the Annual CGT Allowance

Options and warrants allow you to take profits to utilise your annual CGT exemption (worth up to £3,400 per year in saved tax) and avoid falling foul of the taxman's share matching rules. Remember the share matching rules prevent you from selling shares and buying them back for 30 days.

However, there's nothing the Inland Revenue can do if, instead of buying back the shares, you buy options instead. Using options (and spread betting contracts for that matter) you can make sure that you retain your exposure to the underlying asset and make maximum use of the annual CGT exemption.

Delaying the Date of Disposal

Options can be used to delay the date of disposal of a shareholding. Postponing the disposal date provides three key tax benefits:

- You could end up with an extra 12 months to pay capital gains tax, if you manage to push your disposal into the next tax year.
- It can help you make the most of capital losses.
- It allows you to benefit from increased taper relief. For shares treated as non-business assets, an extra 1 year of taper relief will reduce the taxable gain by 5%. For business assets, it could mean a reduction in the gain of 50%.

Example

Denis owns 20,000 shares in Dosh plc. They were acquired in May 2000 for £20,000. Denis decides to sell them for £50,000 in February 2006.

The tax calculation will be as follows:

Proceeds	*£50,000*
Less:	
Cost	*£20,000*
Taper relief @15%	*£4,500*
CGT allowance	*£8,500*
Taxable Gain	*£17,000*
Tax @ 40%	*£6,800*
After-tax proceeds	*£43,200*

The taper relief is 15% because the shares are classed as non-business assets and have been owned for five years. If the disposal date was after May 2006, Denis would have owned the shares for six years, and would therefore obtain taper relief at 20%.

If he believes the price of Dosh shares will drop if he holds them until after May, one possibility would be to obtain put options for £2.80 over 20,000 Dosh plc shares at a premium of 0.15p each.

Let's say the value of the shares has decreased to £45,000 in June 2006 and Denis decides to exercise his option. His gain will be calculated as follows:

Proceeds (£2.8 x 20,000)	*£56,000*
Less:	
Original cost	*£20,000*
Cost of option	*£3,000*
Taper relief @ 20%	*£6,600*
CGT allowance	*£8,500*
Taxable Gain	*£17,900*
Tax @ 40%	*£7,160*
After-tax profits	*£48,840*

Note that in this case, the investor's after-tax profits have increased. He has been able to take advantage of the falling price and also enjoyed an increase in taper relief. Furthermore, the tax payment date has been put back from 31 January 2007 to 31 January 2008. This is an extra 12 months that the CGT will be in his bank or invested and making him more money.

Chapter 8

How to Complete Your Tax Return

Now that we've looked at the rules for calculating capital gains and losses and examined how to take advantage of the many reliefs on offer, it's time to turn our attention to completing the capital gains tax pages of your tax return.

But first it's important to point out that you may not need to declare anything on your tax return.

Firstly, transfers to spouses, which are completely tax free, do not have to be declared.

Secondly, if your gains are within the annual tax-free limit (currently £8,500) AND the total sales proceeds are within the 'notification limit' (currently £34,000), you do not have to declare anything.

The notification limit is simply the annual capital gains tax exemption multiplied by four.

So if you sell shares showing a gain of £8,000 and the total value of the shares is £30,000, the taxman doesn't have to be told.

(By the way, when we say 'gains' we mean taxable profits before taking into account the annual CGT allowance.)

If your gains OR proceeds exceed these limits you need to complete the CGT portion of your tax return. Even if your gains from share disposals are nil, you still need to complete the CGT pages if the total value of the shares exceeds the £34,000 notification limit.

If you incur capital *losses* during the year you do not have to report these to the Inland Revenue unless the disposal value exceeds the notification limit. In practice, you should always declare losses so that they can offset gains in future tax years.

If you are non-UK resident and not ordinarily resident, any gains will be exempt and the capital gains tax pages do not need to be completed (subject to the tax anti-avoidance rules).

If you are claiming reliefs such as rollover relief or gift relief you have to ensure that full details of your disposals are included in the tax return.

And finally, if in any doubt, it's better to disclose than fail to disclose. Failure to report information could see your return being classed as completed 'negligently'. As such, the Inland Revenue could raise a discovery assessment any time for up to six years. By notifying the taxman of your disposals, they cannot usually look back into your affairs further than two years.

Details of your gains and losses are provided in the capital gains supplementary pages – about eight pages in total. These are not automatically provided with the basic tax return and have to be requested from the Inland Revenue.

If you do not automatically receive a tax return from the Inland Revenue you must either request one, along with the CGT supplementary pages, or simply provide the Inland Revenue with all the transaction details by October 5 after the end of the tax year. The Inland Revenue will then provide you with details on how to pay any CGT charge.

The CGT supplementary pages are split into three broad sections. Section one is a simplified one-page form for disposals of quoted shares. Section two is a more detailed form covering disposals of other assets and mixtures of quoted shares and other assets. Section 3 summarizes the disposals and details the final gain arising.

You can either complete a simplified one-page return or a detailed return.

Simplified One-Page Form (CG1)

There are a number of important points to bear in mind about the simplified one-page return:

- It can only be used for transactions in quoted shares or securities (in other words, listed on the London Stock Exchange or an overseas 'recognised stock exchange' throughout the period you held them, or units in a UK authorized unit trust).

- It is of no use if you wish to claim the various CGT reliefs. If you wish to claim taper relief, or gift relief, or EIS relief or you acquired the shares as a result of a share-for-share exchange, or if you acquired them pre-March 1982 you must complete the more detailed CGT pages.

CG1 contains the following columns:

Column A - Details of shares disposed of
Here you will enter the company name, share type (eg, ordinary shares) and number of shares sold.

Column B - Estimate/valuation
You will tick this box if an estimate or valuation of the shares' worth was used. This would be most likely to occur if you transferred the shares to a connected party.

Column C - Date of disposal
Enter the date of disposal of the shares here.

Column D - Disposal proceeds
Enter the total disposal proceeds received (before the offset of any expenses).

Column E - Gain/loss arising
Enter the gain or loss after deducting any indexation relief (only pre-April 1998 purchases qualify for indexation relief).

Column F - Further information

This is used to provide any additional information to the Inland Revenue, for example if the transfer was to a connected party.

You then total up the gains, which go in cell F1, the total losses go in cell F2 and the net gain/loss goes in cell F3.

F4 is used if you have any income tax losses to offset such as trading losses, or losses arising on furnished holiday accommodation. F5 is simply F3-F4.

Cell F6 is used to insert any brought forward capital losses from previous tax years. Remember that brought forward capital losses are only used to reduce the remaining gain to £8,500 - the amount of the annual exemption. Clearly, if at F3, F5 or F7 the gain is less than the annual exemption, no taxable gain will arise.

More Complex Calculations

If you wish to claim taper relief you have to complete pages CG2 and CG3. It should be remembered that there is no mixing of CG1 and CG2 & CG3. You either complete CG1 *or* CG2 & CG3.

If you've held your shares for less than three years there's a good chance you can stick to the simplified CG1 form.

Pages CG2 & CG3 are essentially a double page spreadsheet where you enter all the details of each disposal. The spreadsheet is split up depending on whether your gains are from business assets, non-business assets or a mixture of both. Most stock market investors, except AIM investors are selling non-business assets.

CG2 & CG3 consist of the following columns:

Column A

Provide a brief description of the shares disposed of (company name, type of shares and number of shares disposed of). Remember this now includes all chargeable assets, so you may be including property in here as well.

Column AA

For each disposal you need to include in this column one of the following letters depending on the type of asset disposed of:

Quoted shares/securities	Q
Other shares/securities	U
Land & property	L
Other assets	O

So for most share investors Q is used.

Column B

You will tick this box if you have made any estimates or valuations (mostly relevant if you transferred shares to a 'connected party', as the market value rule would then need to be applied).

Column C

Tick this box if the asset disposed of was acquired before March 31 1982.

Column D

You must enter in here the *later* of the date of acquisition and March 16 1998. This is for taper relief purposes, as non-business assets owned at March 17 1998 are entitled to a 'bonus' year (see Chapter 4).

Column E

Enter the date of disposal of the shares here.

Column F

Enter the total disposal proceeds received before the offset of any expenses, e.g. broker's commission.

Column G

Enter details of any claims that will impact on your gain, *excluding* taper relief and indexation relief. If you don't have enough space, there is a space for additional information at the end of the form so you can simply cross reference to this.

Typical claims will include:

- Rollover relief
- Gift relief
- Negligible value claims
- Rebasing elections (so that for all assets acquired pre-March 1982, the market value at March 31 1982 is automatically used.
- EIS relief

Column H

Here you enter the chargeable gain arising before deducting taper relief or offsetting any losses. There's a special section at the bottom of the page for inserting details of losses.

Column I

Enter 'Bus' in here if any of the assets disposed of are business assets for taper relief purposes. If not, leave blank.

Column J

Enter the applicable taper relief rate, based on whether the asset is a business asset (column I) and the length of ownership (based on columns D and E). The rate entered here will be the percentage of the gain chargeable, eg 85% if the asset has been held for more than five years.

Column K

These columns are for showing the offset of any losses. In Chapter 12 we will show that you are allowed to offset current year losses as you please so as to minimise the overall CGT charge. This is where you would do it.

Column K1 is where you enter the amount of current year capital losses you wish to offset.

Column K2 is used to enter the amount any income tax losses you wish to offset against your gains.

Column K3 is used to state the amount of accumulated losses you have available, brought forward from previous tax years.

Column L

This is simply the gains from column H, less any losses in column K.

Column M

This is where you calculate the net gain after taper relief, by multiplying columns L and J.

The column is then totaled and the total gain is entered in the box at the bottom of the page. This is your total taxable gain (before deducting the annual CGT exemption), which is then used to determine the amount of CGT payable.

Pages CG4, CG5 and CG6 are used where you have disposals of other shares/securities (U), land or property (L) or other assets (O). You are required to provide additional details for each asset disposed of.

Pages CG4, CG5 and CG6 relate normally to unquoted shares and land and property disposals and other assets. Page CG7 is simply a blank page where you can input extra information. This leaves the final page of the capital tax supplementary pages, CG8.

Most of page CG8 asks you to summarise your losses and the rest of the page simply brings all the previous information together and allows you to offset your annual exemption.

The result is your taxable gains which are then added to your other income when you complete the other pages of your tax return.

Deadline

As a general rule, if you have chargeable gains or losses, you will need to complete a tax return for the tax year in question. If you don't input details of your capital losses on the tax return, you would have five years and 10 months from the end of the tax year in which to claim the loss.

For example, a capital loss incurred in tax year 2002/2003 would need to be claimed (in a tax return) by 31 January 2009.

The tax return along with any associated CGT will need to be submitted by 31 January following the tax year in question. If you want Inland Revenue to calculate your tax charge, you'll need to submit the tax return to them by 30 September following the end of the tax year.

Capital gains tax is always payable by 31 January following the end of the tax year. Therefore, for the tax year 6 April 2005 - 5 April 2006, the CGT is due to be paid by 31 January 2007.

Chapter 9

Making the Most of Your Annual CGT Exemption

Regular Annual Disposals – How Do You Do It?

Because the annual CGT allowance is worth up to £3,400 in saved tax each year (£6,800 if you're married), it makes sense to sell shares that are in profit so that the allowance is not wasted.

The problem is you may still want to hold on to the shares because you expect them to rise in value.

It's no longer possible to sell your shares and buy them back immediately (so-called bed and breakfasting). You have to wait 30 days to avoid the anti-avoidance rules (see Chapter 4 on share matching). By then, of course, it may be too late and the shares may have risen in value.

However, there are still ways of getting around the share matching rules:

Bed & Spousing

If you're married one solution is to get your spouse to buy back the shares – also known as 'bed and spousing'.

Example

Bob sells shares with profits of £8,500 in the 2005/2006 tax year and transfers the funds to his wife, Betty, who buys the same shares immediately. Bob's profits are completely tax free and Betty now owns the same shares and can benefit from any price increase.

Note that with any transaction between husband and wife care must be taken to ensure that absolute ownership does pass to the wife and it is not a 'sham arrangement'.

Note this strategy will not work if the shares are owned jointly. For example, Bob and Betty may have bought the shares in joint names so that when the time came to sell they could make use of two annual CGT allowances, instead of just Bob's.

Bed & ISA

An alternative method of avoiding the share matching rules is to repurchase shares through an ISA. The ISA is regarded as the new legal owner in the eyes of the taxman and therefore you can avoid the 30-day matching rule.

Example

Pat has 10,000 shares in Bucks plc. They were originally acquired for £4,000, and have now increased in value to £7,000. He still has his annual CGT exemption for the 2005/2006 tax year available on April 3 2006. He decides to give himself a tax-free uplift in the base cost of his shares by disposing of his entire holding. The gain of £3,000 is covered by his annual exemption and he can then reacquire his shares through a Maxi ISA.

If he did not use the ISA, he would have had to wait 30 days before repurchasing the shares in order to avoid the matching rules. During this period the shares might have increased in value and Pat would have lost out.

Bed & Options or Bed & Spread Bet

There's nothing stopping you from selling your shares to take advantage of your CGT allowance and covering your position for 30 days using either options or other derivatives or a spread betting contract. Naturally you have to know what you're doing but this tactic would completely avoid the share matching rules.

Profits from spread betting are completely tax free, profits from derivatives trades are generally subject to CGT so you would have to do your number crunching and see if the exercise is worthwhile.

Similar Shares or Funds

Let's say you've already used up your ISA allowance, your investments are owned jointly with your spouse and you don't fancy using derivatives or other complicated financial assets. However, you do have some handsome profits and would like to use up your annual CGT allowance.

One option is to simply purchase similar shares or invest in a similar fund. This is, of course, the second-best option but may well be worth considering.

Example

Kathy and Dave jointly own shares in Copper Top plc worth £20,000 which were originally purchased two years ago for £10,000. They sell now and potentially save £4,000 in future capital gains tax (£10,000 profit x 40% tax = £4,000). They decide to invest in Copper Bottom plc for 30 days so they can maintain exposure to the copper market even though this company is not as attractive.

During the 30-day period Copper Top rises 20% and Copper Bottom rises just 10%. In other words, they have lost out on a 10% rise, worth £2,000 (£20,000 Copper Top holding x 10% = £2,000). However, they've saved £4,000 tax so they're still better off.

Whether this strategy is worth following depends critically on whether your profits are large when expressed as a percentage of your total holding. If so, it may well be worth selling now.

It also depends critically on how important to you losing the annual CGT exemption is. You have to decide whether losing this year's CGT allowance will result in a much larger tax bill later on.

This strategy is arguably most suited to unit trust investors, in particular investors in index trackers who can easily substitute one fund for another without losing out on performance.

Sit it Out for 30 Days

Another alternative is to simply sell your investment, wait for 30 days and then reinvest. Here you have to weigh up your tax savings with the potential for the share price to rise.

Example

Kathy and Dave jointly own shares in a company worth £20,000 which were originally purchased two years ago for £10,000. They sell now and, using their CGT exemptions potentially save £4,000 in future capital gains tax. They decide to wait 30 days before buying again to comply with the 30-day rule. In that time the shares jump 10%. In other words, Kathy and Dave have saved £4,000 but lost out on £2,000 of profits. They're still well ahead, however, and the sale was arguably worthwhile.

Whatever you do it's important not to let the tax tail wag the investment dog!

Costs versus Tax Savings

If you sell shares or units in a fund purely to make use of your annual CGT exemption you still have to reinvest the proceeds. This will inevitably result in charges. In the case of shares there is brokerage, marketable securities tax and of course the bid/offer spread.

With unit trusts the costs are potentially far higher. For example many unit trusts levy an initial charge of as much as 5%. In these circumstances, where investment costs are quite high, it is essential to weigh up the costs versus the potential tax savings.

Remember, making use of your £8,500 annual exemption means taking *profits* of £8,500, which may mean selling a considerably far greater amount of shares if your returns are quite low.

Example

John has £100,000 invested in a unit trust. Over the course of the tax year he makes a profit of £8,500 and decides to sell his entire holding to make use of his annual CGT exemption. Doing so he saves himself £3,400 in tax (£8,500 x 40%). He then decides to reinvest in another fund (to avoid the 30-day rule).

Because he has a large amount of capital he is able to get a discount on the initial charge and ends up paying 3% instead of the normal 5%. However he still ends up paying £3,237 in charges, almost completely wiping out his tax savings.

This is an extreme example but proves an important point: selling shares for tax reasons alone can be dangerous especially when costs are high or you have to dispose of a large block of shares to use all your CGT allowance.

CGT Exemption and Taper Relief

The problem with selling shares to take advantage of your annual capital gains tax allowance is that the taper relief 'clock' is reset to zero. Remember the amount of taper relief you get depends on how long you hold your assets. After 10 years 40% of your gains are tax free.

If you're a long-term investor it often doesn't make sense to sell shares frequently, if at all, to use up your annual CGT exemption.

Example

Jimmy and Annabel, both higher-rate taxpayers, invest £30,000 in blue chips for 10 years, earning a respectable return of 7% per year. After 10 years they have almost doubled their money and earned a profit of £29,015.

The tax calculation is pretty simple. Thanks to taper relief 40% of their profits (£11,606) is completely tax free. That leaves profits of £17,409. Because they qualify for two capital gains tax allowances and because this allowance is likely to grow by at least £300 per year, we can safely say that in 10 years' time the combined allowance will be worth at least £19,700.

This means that the profits of £17,409 left after deducting taper relief will be completely tax free.

In summary, they have invested £30,000, doubled their money over 10 years and not paid a penny in capital gains tax!

This example shows that an investor with a reasonable sum of money can invest for a long period of time and not pay much tax. However, tweak the numbers and you get a very different outcome.

For example, if Jimmy and Annabel had £100,000 to invest instead of £30,000 they would end up with a tax bill of £15,332. Or if they had earned 15% instead of 7% they would have ended up with a tax bill of £14,048.

So many long-term investors will have to take profits every now and then (but not necessarily every year) to minimise their capital gains tax bills.

Chapter 10

How Your Spouse Can Help Cut Your Tax Bill

It's one of the most important tax breaks available and you should always think of ways of exploiting it:

Spouses can transfer shares or other assets to each other without paying any capital gains tax.

There are several reasons why you may wish to transfer assets to a spouse. Firstly, if the assets generate income it makes sense for the spouse with the lowest tax rate to earn it (see Chapter 21 on income splitting with your spouse).

Secondly, if you want to sell some shares it makes sense to hold shares jointly so both spouses can exploit the annual capital gains tax allowance.

But that's not all. In fact, in certain circumstances this is not even the main tax break. When we say it makes sense to hold shares jointly we don't mean 50:50, unless the husband and wife earn similar amounts of income and gains.

If one is a basic-rate taxpayer or earns little or no income and there are big capital gains that exceed the two annual allowances, it makes sense for the spouse with the lowest income to own a greater proportion of the assets.

The profits that exceed the CGT exemption will be taxed at 10% or 20%, rather than 40%. This could generate further tax savings of over £6,000.

Example

Frank buys 10,000 shares in Fastgrow plc in 2000 for £1 each. They're now worth £40,000. If he sells them, taper relief will exempt 15% of the profits and a further £8,500 will be exempted by the annual CGT allowance. This will leave £17,000 of taxable profits and a total tax bill of £6,800 if Frank is a higher rate taxpayer.

If instead he transferred shares to his wife Fiona who doesn't earn any income he could reduce the tax bill drastically.

The shares are showing a profit of £3 per share so if Frank keeps hold of shares with £8,500 worth of profits (approximately 2,833 shares) there will be no tax payable when he sells his holding. All the profits will be taken care of by the annual CGT exemption.

His wife Fiona receives the remaining 7,167 shares and her tax calculation is as follows:

Proceeds 7,167 x £4	*£28,668*
Less:	
Acquisition cost 7,167 x £1	*£7,167*
Less CGT allowance	*£8,500*
Taxable gain	*£13,001*
£2,090 @ 10%	*£209*
£10,911 @ 20%	*£2,182.20*
Total Tax	*£2,391.20*

The total tax bill has fallen from £6,800 to £2,391.20 because the couple made use of the two annual CGT exemptions AND Fiona's starting-rate and basic-rate tax bands.

What this example illustrates is that, not only is it worthwhile for spouses to split assets, the 50:50 split is not always the best option. If one of the spouses earns little or no income it's worth transferring an even greater share to that person.

Making the Most of Losses

The tax break for inter-spouse transfer can also be used to make the most of capital losses.

Example

Joe is married to Jenna. Joe has shares in ABC plc standing at a gain of £25,000 (after all reliefs). Jenna has a capital loss of £35,000 from a disposal of a number of her shares a number of years ago.

In order to eliminate his CGT charge, Joe could simply transfer the shares to Jenna. Jenna could then dispose of the shares and offset her old capital loss against the current year's capital gain.

The Legal Stuff

Note that under present law, this rule applies only to married couples and they must be living together for at least part of the tax year in question. The Government has stated that it plans to review the position of co-habiting couples and same sex couples, with a view to giving them similar rights.

For tax purposes a husband and wife are treated as 'living together' unless they are:

- Separated under a court order or separation deed, or
- Separated in circumstances which render permanent separation likely

Example

Pete and Petra decide to separate in August 2005. The decree absolute is awarded in September 2007. Pete and Petra can make transfers for the whole of the 2005/2006 tax year even though they are not 'living together' from August 2005. (Although it's anyone's guess why they would want to transfer assets to each other!)

For the 2006/2007 tax year they will not have been living together during any part of the tax year and therefore tax-free transfers cannot be made. Instead, it is likely that Pete and Petra will be regarded as 'connected parties' (see Chapter 4) and capital gains tax will be payable based on the full market value of the assets transferred.

For periods after the decree absolute is awarded, the normal CGT rules will apply.

Watch Out For Income Tax

The transfer of shares to a spouse applies not only for capital gains tax purposes but for income tax and inheritance tax too.

Example

Jack is married to Jill. Jack is a basic-rate taxpayer and Jill is a higher rate taxpayer. Jack owns shares in XYZ plc and decides to transfer half his shareholding to his wife in order that two annual exemptions can be utilised when the shares are eventually sold.

The problem with this is that if XYZ plc has a high dividend yield any dividends will be taxed in Jack and Jill's hands equally, although Jack will pay no income tax as he is a basic-rate taxpayer, and Jill will pay an effective 25%.

Therefore if they both received £5,000 of dividends, Jill would pay £1,250 income tax. If the shares had been retained by Jack no income tax would be payable.

So in this case joint ownership confers a capital gains tax benefit but an income tax penalty.

Inland Revenue Election

Where assets are held jointly by spouses the general rule is that the Inland revenue would treat you each as being entitled to 50% of the income. This is irrespective of the actual ownership, and this could work to your advantage. For example, if a higher earning spouse actually enjoys 90% of the income, he could only be taxed on 50% of the income.

If you wish to split income in any other proportion, you are permitted to submit an election to Inland Revenue stating what proportion you each own. This is known as an s282B election. Therefore if you wanted to be taxed on 90% of the dividends with your wife taxed on the remaining 10%, you could make this election and the Inland Revenue would accept this.

Note that this proportion would then usually be taken as the ownership for CGT purposes and care would need to be taken when considering whether to make the election.

There were changes to the application of these rules in the 2004 Budget but only as regards shares in close companies (these are companies that are controlled by the directors or only a few shareholders – eg family companies). For these companies the assumption of a 50:50 split is not made, and the income would be taxed on the actual entitlement.

Transfers and CGT

In order to minimise any adverse income tax consequences you may think it's best to simply transfer shares immediately prior to a disposal.

However, transferring shares to a spouse to minimise CGT needs to be approached with caution. It is advisable that the final disposal does not take place just after the interspouse transfer. It is possible that anti-avoidance provisions could be invoked by Inland Revenue.

Frequently, husband and wife transfers are made with little supporting documentation. As a minimum, a transfer of the beneficial interest should be undertaken, and in this case supporting evidence should include a signed and dated deed of gift.

For added certainty, should the Inland Revenue enquire into the matter, you may decide to amend the share certificates showing the joint ownership of the shares.

The transfer should be a reality and not merely an artificial exercise which Inland Revenue could argue is a 'sham'.

The spouse receiving the shares should therefore, for all intents and purposes, be the owner of the shares and have the normal rights of ownership. For example, on the eventual disposal of the shares the funds should not be immediately channelled back to the original spouse holding the shares.

Chapter 11

How Your Children Can Help Cut Your Tax Bill

It's possible to gift your children shares or cash to buy shares and any profits will be taxed in *their* hands, allowing full use to be made of their annual capital gains tax exemptions. Children of *all ages* qualify for an annual CGT exemption.

There are, however, traps to watch out for when gifting shares or other assets to children:

- When you transfer the shares you will have to pay capital gains tax because transfers to children are classed as 'disposals' for CGT purposes. So caution has to be exercised when transferring shares which are already showing handsome profits or if you've already made use of your own CGT exemption for the year.

- A gift to a minor child of shares where the dividend income is more than £100 per tax year will be caught by Inland Revenue's anti-avoidance rules. Although from a capital gains tax standpoint the child would own the shares, the dividends would continue to be taxed in the hands of the gifting parent.

- Inheritance tax consequences (see Chapter 22).

Capital Gains Tax Savings

Despite the above drawbacks, gifting assets to children is an extremely effective long-term capital gains tax saving strategy.

CGT can be avoided when you initially make the gift by, for example, only gifting shares which have recently been acquired and have relatively small gains. You can also make sure you gift shares in years in which your CGT exemption is available.

Income tax on dividends can be avoided simply by gifting shares that don't pay income or which have very low dividend yields!

For parents who are 40% taxpayers, this could result in useful tax savings. For example, gains of up to £8,500 per tax year will be completely tax free, and provided the proceeds are less than £34,000 the gain will not have to be disclosed on a tax return.

Example

Jane and Steve, both higher rate taxpayers, jointly own £30,000 of China Bucks plc shares which are showing gains of £10,000. They gift the shares to their eight-year-old son, Steve jr, and their five-year-old daughter, Abi.

There will be no CGT payable if Jane and Steve's annual CGT exemptions have not been used up in the year the gift is made. We'll also assume that these are high growth shares which do not pay dividends so Jane and Steve don't have to worry about paying any income tax.

Let's say that over the next 10 years the shares rise in value to £70,000 and are sold to pay for the children's university studies. We'll also assume the annual CGT exemption has risen in value to £11,000.

The children will be each taxed as follows:

Proceeds	*£35,000*
Less cost	*£15,000*
Gain	*£20,000*
Less taper relief @ 40%	*£8,000*
Tapered gain	*£12,000*
Less CGT Exemption	*£11,000*
Taxable gain	*£1,000*
Tax @ 10%	*£100*

So the combined tax bill for Steve jr and Abi on £40,000 of profits is £200. What's more, the parents still have their annual exemptions free for other disposals.

Note, transferring shares to children is only worthwhile as a capital gains tax planning tool if you and your spouse have significant assets and value your annual exemptions highly.

Where there is only one child, remember that in many cases you will be substituting two annual exemptions (yours and your spouse's) for one annual exemption (the child's).

So it is possible to transfer shares and end up paying *more* capital gains tax!

The Legal Stuff

Care needs to be taken with the legal formalities regarding capacity to enter contracts and it may simply be necessary to transfer the beneficial interest to the child.

As it is the beneficial interest that determines who will be taxed, the child would in theory suffer the CGT charge on an eventual disposal.

It would be sensible in this situation to draw up a deed of bare trust. This would state that the parent holds the legal title to the shares, but the full beneficial entitlement rests with the child.

The gift would also be a potentially exempt transfer for inheritance tax purposes (see Chapter 22). However, provided the parent survives seven years after making the gift, the value will be excluded from the estate for IHT purposes.

If the parent was to survive less than seven years, all or part of the value of the gift would be included in the parent's estate.

Note that any transfer to a child would be most tax efficient where the gift was of shares with a low inbuilt gain and you expect the shares to grow strongly in the years ahead.

The gain on transfer would then be low and, in addition, for IHT purposes, the shares' valuation would be fixed at the date of transfer, which may be substantially lower than the probate value.

It's also possible to avoid the anti-avoidance rules on dividend income if grandparents, instead of parents gift assets. So it's possible to arrange for shares or other assets that generate high income to be transferred into the names of the children (or more sensibly into some form of trust for them) and all the income will be taxed in the children's (or trust's) hands.

The income would probably be covered by the children's personal allowances or taxed at a lower rate in the hands of the trust.

Chapter 12

How to Make the Most of Your Losses

If you dispose of shares for less than their original cost, a capital loss arises. The general rule is that a capital loss can be offset against capital gains you have made in the *current* tax year.

If you still have losses left over, these can be carried forward and offset against gains made in future tax years.

The important point to note is that losses incurred in a *previous* tax year are only used to reduce your current year's chargeable gains down to £8,500, the amount of the annual capital gains tax exemption.

This is good news because it prevents the annual CGT exemption from being wasted.

Example

Justin, a higher rate taxpayer, made the following share transactions:

- *July 1 2005 sold shares in PT plc and made a gain of £12,000.*

- *April 1 2005 sold shares in GF plc and suffered a loss of £10,000.*

The loss of £10,000 is offset against the gain of £12,000 (as these occurred in the same tax year), leaving a net gain of £2,000. Assuming no taper relief is due, the tax position would be as follows:

Gain	*£12,000*
Less: loss	*£10,000*
Less: Annual exemption £8,500 but restricted to	*£2,000*
Taxable Gain	*NIL*

As no other gains occurred during the tax year £6,500 of the annual exemption is effectively wasted. But if the loss of £10,000 was incurred in the ***previous*** *tax year, and carried forward to the current 2005/2006 tax year, only £3,500 of the loss would be offset:*

Gain	*£12,000*
Less: Loss	*£3,500*
Less: Annual exemption	*£8,500*
Gain	*NIL*

The remaining £6,500 of losses can be carried forward to the next tax year and potentially result in a tax saving of £2,600 (40% of £6,500).

Because losses carried forward are worth more than losses written off in the current tax year, the crucial question is, how do you ensure your losses are carried forward rather than used up in the current tax year?

Sell Loss-Making Shares

One way of maximising the benefit is to sell loss-making shares in a year when you have no other capital gains.

Example

Bill has £10,000 profit showing on Bull plc and a £10,000 loss showing on Bear plc. If he sells them in the same tax year he will pay no capital gains tax but will also waste most of his annual CGT exemption. If instead he just sells Bear plc he will make a loss of £10,000. This loss will be carried forward to the next tax year. Let's say in this next tax year he sells Bull plc. The tax calculation will be as follows:

Gain	*£10,000*
Less:	
Previous year's loss	*£1,500*
Less:	
Annual exemption	*£8,500*
Taxable Gain	*NIL*

And he still has £8,500 of losses to carry forward to future tax years!

Married Couples

Another way of making the most of losses is to ensure that loss-making shares are *not* owned jointly. As we've already discussed, it often makes sense for married couples to own shares jointly so that they can make full use of two annual CGT exemptions and the starting and basic-rate tax bands. With losses the opposite is sometimes true. To ensure losses can be carried forward it often pays for only one spouse to own the shares.

Example

Bill and Wendy have £5,000 of profits showing on Bull plc and £5,000 of losses showing on Bear plc. They want to dispose of both holdings in the current tax year. If they sell both, the gain from Bull will be offset by the loss from Bear and no tax will be payable. However, they will also waste their annual capital gains tax exemptions. If instead Bill owns and sells Bull plc and Wendy owns and sells Bear plc, Bill will not have to pay any tax because his gain will be covered by his annual CGT exemption. Wendy's £5,000 loss will be carried forward to future tax years.

Alternatively they could sell Bear plc now and Bull plc in the new tax year, just as in the previous example. This may have the same tax consequences but may not be a desirable investment strategy.

Chapter 13

Getting Extra Mileage from Your ISAs

The humble ISA is one of the most powerful tools in the private investor's toolkit. Effectively a couple can invest £14,000 per tax year and shelter all their income and capital gains forever more from the taxman.

However, there's more to ISAs than meets the eye. In this chapter we explain all the rules and, more importantly, show you how ISAs can be utilised to achieve extra tax savings.

Investment Limits

For the current 2005/2006 tax year you can invest £7,000 in an equity 'Maxi ISA' and £3,000 in a cash ISA.

In the 2005 Budget it was announced that these limits will remain until at least 2010.

Investors must be aged 18 or over to own share ISAs (16-18 to own cash ISAs).

Investment Options

You can use ISAs to invest in a wide variety of different assets:

- Shares and corporate bonds issued by companies listed on recognised stock exchanges anywhere in the world.

- UK gilts and government bonds issued by other countries in the European Economic Area.

- Units in UK authorised unit trusts or open ended investment companies (OEICs).

- Shares in approved investment trusts.

- Units or shares in 'Undertakings for Collective Investment in Transferable Securities' (UCITS) funds based elsewhere in the European Union (these are similar to UK authorised unit trusts and OEICS).

- Any shares which have been transferred from an Inland Revenue approved employee share scheme.

Note that options and warrants cannot be held within an ISA.

Also, only quoted shares can be included. This includes Techmark shares but shares treated as unquoted for tax purposes (for example, shares listed on the Alternative Investment Market) cannot be included within an ISA, unless they are received through a qualifying employee share scheme.

You also cannot put shares you inherit into an ISA or any other existing shares that you already own. There is, however, one exception to this rule. You are allowed to invest certain shares obtained through an employee share scheme.

You would need to transfer shares emerging from a SAYE scheme or an approved Profit Share Scheme directly into the ISA within 90 days of exercising the option. This would then enable you to avoid CGT altogether. The usual limits would still apply, so for a maxi ISA the value of the shares at the date of transfer would need to be less than £7,000.

Losses

Just as any gains from ISA investments are not taxable, so any losses are not available for offset against other gains.

Non-residency

If you become non resident you are not allowed to continue investing in an ISA. However, Inland Revenue will allow you to keep your ISA investments and they will still obtain the beneficial tax treatment (eg dividends exempt from UK income tax). On your return to the UK, you can then continue to top up your ISA investments.

Using Your Spouse

Spouses are treated independently for tax purposes and therefore each spouse is entitled to invest up to £7,000 per tax year. This means a married couple could invest £14,000 on April 4 2006, and another £14,000 on April 6 2006.

It rarely pays not to use up your ISA allowance as there are generally no penalties, minimum investment periods or other hidden costs.

Using Your Children

There's nothing to stop you gifting cash to your adult children so that they can have their own ISAs. All income and capital gains will be completely tax free.

Remember this could be a potentially exempt transfer for inheritance tax purposes and taxed as part of your estate if you die within seven years (see Chapter 22 on inheritance tax planning). However, the first £3,000 of donations per person per tax year are completely exempt from inheritance tax.

The Benefits of Self-select ISAs

Self-select ISAs are ideal for active investors. They let you buy and sell shares as often as you like.

They're available from stockbrokers, including online stockbrokers and certain high street banks.

When picking the best plan you have to look out for charges and restrictions on what kind of shares can be bought and sold (for example, can you invest internationally or only in UK shares?).

Self-select ISAs are usually more expensive than ordinary ISAs. You have to compare annual charges which can range from 0.5% to 1.5% per year. There may also be minimum charges for every deal.

You also have to have faith in the firm's ability to handle your trades quickly and efficiently.

Tax Tip

So should you use a self-select ISA? Naturally, if all you do is trade shares a self-select ISA is essential. But what if you regularly trade shares and also have long-term holdings – should you use your ISA allowance to protect your long-term investments or your short-term trades?

The answer depends critically on whether your annual trading profits currently exceed your annual CGT allowance (£8,500 if you're single, £17,000 if you're married).

If they do, then it almost certainly pays to use a self-select ISA for trading purposes and invest your long–term holdings directly in shares or unit trusts.

Why? Because if your annual trading profits exceed the CGT allowance they will definitely be taxed. By its very nature trading means you are making disposals which give rise to CGT. But tax will be completely avoided on capital that is sheltered by a self-select ISA.

In contrast, if your 'paper' profits from your long-term holdings exceed the annual CGT allowance they will not be taxed until you make a disposal, by which time they may qualify for 40% taper relief, with the balance being offset by your annual capital gains tax allowance.

What if your annual trading profits do not exceed your annual CGT allowance?

If you trade through an ISA and your profits are less than £8,500 (£17,000 if married) you will not receive any immediate tax benefit because your profits are already tax free. However, if you enjoy success and your profits grow you will eventually pay CGT so a self-select ISA is arguably still worth considering. Your long-term holdings will then be invested directly but again will not be subject to CGT until you sell, by which time they could be covered by taper relief and the annual CGT allowance.

The only drawback with using a self-select ISA as a frequent trader is that you are limited to the amount of capital you can invest. If you have a substantial trading portfolio you will then end up with some of your trades done through an ISA and the others done directly. This will result in multiple orders, possibly with multiple brokers and may be more trouble than it's worth. In these cases, especially if your profits are well below the annual CGT exemption, it may be worth using an ISA to protect your long-term investments.

Equities vs Bonds

If you have a balanced portfolio with some of your money in shares and the rest in gilts and corporate bonds, it may be worth considering whether it's your bonds or your shares that are sheltered in ISAs. Because most of the return from bonds comes in the form of taxable interest, it probably makes sense to use an ISA to protect these investments rather than shares. Equity returns, on the other hand, come mainly in the form of capital growth which qualifies for taper relief and the annual CGT exemption.

You should arguably only use your ISA allowance to shelter equities if you expect them to generate significantly higher returns than your bonds over time.

How Should You Use Your ISA Savings?

Some investors use ISAs to save for a specific eventuality, such as paying for a child's education. This is arguably not a good idea because once you sell your ISAs the tax benefits are lost forever.

If you're saving to pay for a future expense there's a very good chance that by investing directly in equities or unit trusts, rather than using an ISA wrapper, you will pay little or no capital gains tax anyway, leaving your precious ISA allowance free to put to better uses.

Example 1

Dave and Sue inherit £28,000 and decide to invest in an equity unit trust (note, not an ISA) for 10 years. After that they intend to use most of the funds to pay for their children's education. They enjoy annual returns of 7% per year. After 10 years the fund will be worth £55,080 with a total profit of £27,080. How much tax will they pay? Taper relief at 40% will protect £10,832 of their profits and the remaining £16,248 will easily be covered by their two annual CGT exemptions.

So even though Dave and Sue invested a sizeable chunk of money and earned a respectable return, they did not pay a penny in tax on their profits. If Dave and Sue had used an ISA instead they would have derived absolutely no tax benefit.

Where ISAs really come into their own is where you hold on to them for many years and use them to generate tax-free income when you retire.

Example 2

Dave and Sue decide to invest their £28,000 in an ISA for a period of 20 years to fund their retirements. Based on the same growth assumptions as the previous example, after 20 years the investment will be worth £108,351. They now wish to retire and switch from a growth fund to an income-focused fund (ISA umbrella funds, for example, allow you to invest in different funds provided by different managers and switch from one to the other). The income fund has a yield of 6%, delivering them a tax-free income of £6,501 per year.

If instead of using an ISA Dave and Sue had invested directly the outcome would be entirely different. First of all the switch from a growth fund to an income fund would result in a capital gains tax charge (in this case £7,924). This means they have less capital to invest for income and so their income will be just £6,026. However that's not the end of the story. There's still tax to pay on this income. Assuming half comes from share dividends and half comes from bond interest their after-tax income will be just £4,067.

Hence by using an ISA they end up with 60% more income than by investing directly in unit trusts.

The important lessons to learn from this example are that:

- ISAs allow you, in certain circumstances, to switch between different investment funds without paying any tax. This is very valuable if you want to rebalance your portfolio every now and again.

- ISAs are most effective when held for the long term with a view to ultimately generating retirement income.

Chapter 14

Spread Betting: a Fantastic Tax Shelter

More and more investors are being lured by the attractions of spread betting as a means of making money on financial markets. Spread betting offers the following benefits:

- You can bet on both rising and falling markets.
- It's easy to bet on quite exotic instruments such as foreign stock market indexes.
- You can leverage your capital by placing a big bet with only a small initial outlay.

Spread betting is also probably the most tax-efficient way of making money on financial markets, for two major reasons:

- There is no capital gains tax on profits.
- There is no stamp duty payable.

The capital gains tax exemption is the all-important factor for most speculators. Spread betting is not a viable alternative to long-term share investment, however. Spread betters cannot ride out the ups and downs of the stock market and cannot use their betting activities to generate dividend income.

However, the tax breaks make it a serious option for frequent traders/speculators.

Example

It's the beginning of the tax year and Conrad and Rupert both have £10,000 to speculate on share price movements over a 12-month period.

Conrad is a spread better, Rupert invests directly in the stock market. Let's say both are incredibly lucky and call the market correctly each time and end up with profits of £20,000 after 12 months. Because he's a spread better, Conrad will have no tax to pay. Rupert has the same pre-tax profits but will end up with a tax bill of £4,600. (We've softened the tax blow by assuming that he can make full use of his annual CGT exemption.)

Clearly this example is simplistic. It ignores Rupert's dealing costs and the premium Conrad has to pay to place his bets. It also assumes that Conrad has not 'geared up' his positions. In other words, if the shares rise by 20% his return is 20% and not some multiple of that. However, these factors do not detract from the all important point:

A successful spread better will end up with much more money than a successful share speculator.

It could be argued that spread betters shoulder much more risk than normal investors. The risk in spread betting comes from several quarters, in particular the time limit on bets and the potentially unlimited downside. These risks can be controlled to some extent by the serious speculator looking for a serious alternative to buying shares or other securities directly.

What is not so well documented is the fact that, because of their unequal tax treatment, spread betting can be *less* risky than direct share investment. Let's return to Conrad and Rupert to see why.

So far Rupert, the share investor, has been reinvesting all of his profits in new trades, even though up to 40 per cent of each month's profit belongs to the taxman. There is no risk in doing this, *provided all the trades fall within the same tax year.* Remember the capital gains tax rules let you offset gains made in one year against losses made in the same tax year.

If Rupert suddenly makes big losses he can offset these against profits from previous months' trades without any danger of having insufficient funds to settle his annual capital gains tax bill. However, when the trading straddles two *separate* tax years it's a completely different story. Rupert cannot offset losses made in one year against gains made in the *previous* tax year.

If Rupert uses all his profits from the previous tax year to buy shares at the beginning of the next tax year he is taking a big risk because he is trading with money that does not belong to him but to the taxman.

Alternatively, if he plays it safe and only reinvests his after-tax profits, his returns will be much lower than Conrad's.

Example

It's the beginning of the next tax year and both Conrad and Rupert have £30,000 in their trading accounts (the original £10,000 plus £20,000 of profits). However, there is an important difference. Rupert has a tax bill of £4,600 that has to be settled when he submits his tax return. So in reality he only has £25,400 of his own money with which to speculate. Assuming they earn the same returns as before, Conrad will end up with £90,000 and Rupert will end up with just £76,200. Rupert is falling behind because he has less capital to invest during the current year. However, that's not the end of the story. Rupert has to pay tax on these profits as well, leaving him with just £59,280.

In summary, both Conrad and Rupert invested in the same shares and earned identical pre-tax returns. However, because Conrad went the spread betting route he ended up with 52% more money!

When Spread Betting is Not Worthwhile

- If your annual trading profits are under £8,500 (or £17,000 in the case of married couples), the spread betting tax break is largely irrelevant as your capital gains will be completely tax free anyway. So only serious traders, or those with significant other capital gains, should consider spread betting purely for tax reasons. As can be seen throughout this book, the humble CGT allowance can throw a lot of clever tax planning ideas on their head.

- There has been some speculation in the financial press in recent times that the Chancellor may be considering taxing spread betting profits. There is also the perceived danger that an individual who is regarded as carrying out a 'trading activity' will fall into the income tax net, even if the profits arise from spread betting. There is no guidance on this issue, and the Inland Revenue has not, to my knowledge, raised this argument yet. The circumstances where such an argument would be raised are likely to be exceptional and the average individual engaging in spread betting would not be at risk.

- It is also worth emphasizing the potential risks of spread betting. For one, there is frequently no loss limit. With a holding of shares the most the investor can lose is the original stake. Spread betters could lose much more than this, although some transactions do offer a stop loss facility.

Summary

- Spread betting profits are completely free of capital gains tax.

- Spread betting transactions are not subject to stamp duty. Ordinary share investors pay 0.5% stamp duty on all purchases.

- Spread betting is a high-risk activity but nevertheless a viable alternative to short-term share speculation.

- Spread betting is not a viable alternative for the long-term investor, especially those wanting to earn income.

- Spread betters can reinvest profits from one tax year to the next. Prudent share speculators have to make provision for capital gains tax.

Chapter 15

Unit Trusts: Another Great Tax Shelter

As we saw in Chapter 5, unit trusts, OEICs and investment trusts are generally taxed in the same way as direct share investments. Profits on any disposal are subject to tax after subtracting taper relief and the annual capital gains tax allowance.

However, authorized investment funds such as these do offer one interesting tax break: The fund does not *itself* pay tax on its capital gains. This means the manager of the fund can buy and sell shares to his heart's content without any capital gains tax being payable from year to year. It's only when *you* sell your units/shares in the fund that tax becomes payable. This means your investment can grow tax free over many years.

In contrast, if you manage your own portfolio (or employ a professional manager such as a stockbroker), capital gains tax will potentially be payable every time you make a disposal.

So if you are happy to entrust all or part of your money to a professional fund manager there is scope to make tax savings by investing via an authorized unit trust, OEIC or investment trust. The critical questions are, *who* benefits most from this tax break and *how much* tax are you likely to save?

Those investors most likely to benefit are those who are already making full use of their annual capital gains tax exemptions and their ISA allowances. This is pretty obvious – if your profits are easily covered by the annual CGT exemption or sheltered in an ISA, tax is not a worry. However, if your annual stock market profits (or other capital gains for that matter) regularly exceed the exemption, you may benefit by investing some of your money in an authorised investment fund. The theory is that, if the fund is well managed, your investment will continue to grow as much as before and there will be no annual tax bill, leaving more left over for reinvestment.

Of course you could simply buy shares directly and hold on to them. The problem here is that, unlike the fund manager, you will not be able to make the inevitable adjustments that every well-managed portfolio requires.

So how much tax are you likely to save by investing in a unit trust compared with investing directly? That depends on a number of assumptions, including how much investment capital you have, how long you are prepared to invest, your expected returns and how frequently you take profits. Almost every conceivable factor in other words! Although this issue is potentially complex it is worth taking time to investigate as, in the right circumstances, it could result in a large increase in your after-tax returns.

Let's examine a couple of examples.

Example 1

Paul and Steve are both higher rate taxpayers and both are making full use of their annual CGT exemptions. Paul invests £10,000 in an aggressively managed unit trust for 10 years and enjoys capital growth of 10% per year. To keep matters simple we'll assume there are no dividends. Steve invests £10,000 directly in shares, selling at the end of each year and reinvesting in new companies.

After 10 years Paul, the unit trust investor, will own an investment worth £25,937. If he sells his units his capital gain will be £15,937 (£25,937 - £10,000). From this he can deduct 40% taper relief because he has held the units for more than 10 years. Taper relief comes to £6,375, leaving him with £9,562 on which he has to pay tax at 40%. This leaves him with a total fund of £22,112 after tax.

What about Steve? He sells his shares each year and, assuming he has already fully utilised his annual exemption, pays 40% tax on his total profits, without enjoying any taper relief – remember this relief only kicks in after three years. After year 10 he will be left with just £17,908.

Paul and Steve have both earned identical pre-tax returns but Paul, the unit trust investor, ends up with 23% more money.

A lot of the difference can be explained by the fact that Paul gets 40% taper relief, whereas Steve gets nothing. However, this is only part of the story. If we ignore this relief and assume that Paul, the unit trust investor, also pays 40% tax on *all* his profits (with the critical difference that he only pays tax at the *end* of the investment period), he still ends up well ahead. In this instance his fund will be worth £19,562 compared with Steve's £17,908. Paul ends up with 9% more money even though they both earned the same pre-tax returns AND paid 40% tax on all their profits.

The difference in returns can be explained by the fact that Paul has been able to reinvest 100% of his profits each year and let compound growth work its magic. Money that Steve has had to pay to the taxman, Paul has been able to reinvest to generate more profits! Steve, on the other hand, has only been able to reinvest 60% of his profits so the compound growth effect has been somewhat diminished.

Because unit trust investors can potentially reinvest the taxman's money for longer periods of time, another critical question is: "How sensitive are these results to the length of the investment period?" What we will see is that the longer you invest, the more important the unit trust tax break becomes.

Example 2

The facts are exactly the same as before except this time the investment period is 20 years. Now Paul, the unit trust investor ends up with £53,529 after accounting for 40% taper relief and tax on the remainder. Steve, the share investor who pays tax every year, ends up with £32,071.

This time Paul's fund is 67% bigger than Steve's! Paul ends up better off because he enjoys 40% taper relief but, most importantly, because he only has to pay tax at the end of the investment period when he cashes in his unit trust.

Unit Trusts vs Direct Investment

If you are an experienced and successful investor and only investing in unit trusts for *tax* reasons you could argue that you will still be better off investing directly in shares because your returns will be far higher, even if you have to pay more tax. This is certainly an important argument against using unit trusts for tax reasons. The critical question is, how much better do your returns have to be to beat the unit trust?

In the above 10-year example, if Steve the direct share investor, managed to earn 14% per year, after tax he would end up slightly better off than Paul, the unit trust investor, who only earns 10% per year.

So, as we've pointed out several times throughout this guide, it is always dangerous to base your investment decisions on tax factors alone! Nevertheless the unit trust tax break is an interesting and potentially important one for serious investors who are already making full use of their annual capital gains tax and ISA allowances.

Chapter 16

Making the Most of Taper Relief

Most shares, unit trusts and other financial assets that fall into the capital gains tax net only qualify for the less generous non-business asset taper relief. Non-business taper only kicks in after three years and is capped at 40% after ten years. With business taper, on the other hand, 75% of your capital gains are tax free after just two years! For those that qualify it's an incredibly generous tax break.

The favoured few who qualify include:

- The entrepreneurial – those who own shares in unquoted trading companies.
- The rich – who can afford to buy more than 5% of a quoted company.
- The risk lovers – those prepared to invest in AIM shares.
- The lucky – those whose employers happen to be quoted companies.

So how much is this tax break worth? To find out let's examine each category of shareholder in turn.

The Entrepreneurial

Starting with the entrepreneurs, let's say you've spent the last three years building a profitable IT company. You now decide to sell your shares for £250,000 and do something else; for example start another company! Of that £250,000 only £62,500 (25%) falls into the tax net. Subtracting another £8,500 in respect of the annual CGT allowance leaves you with just £54,000 subject to tax. If you're a higher-rate taxpayer the total tax bill would be just £21,600 – an *effective* tax rate of just 8.6%!

That's why building and selling companies is arguably the most tax-efficient way of making money. Essentially by selling a company you are converting taxable profits (the future profits of the business) into low tax capital gains.

However, the main focus of this guide is the tax treatment of *quoted* companies so we will not explore the first category any further.

The Rich

We will also largely ignore the second category, those with shareholdings in excess of 5%. After all, how many people do you know who own more than 5% of a quoted company?

The Risk Lovers and The Lucky

We all know that AIM shares are not for the faint hearted. They enjoyed meteoric rises during the dot com bubble and then came crashing down after 2000.

For the speculative investor they remain a serious alternative to other small companies, especially since they qualify for business asset taper relief. The criticial question is: "Should I buy shares in an AIM company just to exploit the business taper tax break?"
The same question might be asked by employees of listed companies.

Surely 75% of profits tax free after just two years compared with 0% for most other shares makes them seriously worthy of consideration? To answer that question we analysed after-tax returns from business assets (AIM shares and employer company shares) and non-business assets (most other shares) over different time periods to see how they compare. The results are summarised in the table on the next page.

Business Assets vs Other Shares

%	Years 1	2	3	4	5	6	7	8	9	10
10	8	7	7	7	7	8	8	8	8	8
20	15	13	14	14	15	15	16	16	16	17
30	23	20	21	21	22	23	23	24	25	25
40	30	27	28	28	29	30	31	32	33	34
50	38	33	34	36	37	38	39	40	41	42
60	45	40	41	43	44	45	47	48	49	51
70	53	47	48	50	51	53	54	56	58	59
80	60	53	55	57	59	60	62	64	66	68
90	68	60	62	64	66	68	70	72	74	76
100	75	67	69	71	73	76	78	80	82	84

In this table the figures in bold are pre-tax returns from non-business assets (normal quoted shares). The top row of the table is years. The rest of the numbers are equivalent pre-tax returns from shares that qualify for business asset taper relief.

For example, if an ordinary share investor earns a pre-tax return of 30% after two years, an AIM investor only has to earn 20% to walk away with the same after-tax profits.

Clearly, from a tax-planning perspective, shares that qualify for business taper relief are an attractive alternative to other quoted company shares. Whether they're a good all-round investment is another story!

It's also important to note that not all AIM company shares qualify for business asset taper relief. The companies in question still need to be proper 'trading companies'.

This means they must not be involved in 'substantial' non-trading activities. 'Substantial' for this purpose means that the company must not have more than 20% of its turnover, assets or workforce in a non-trading capacity.

The definition of 'non trading' is potentially wide but is most likely to consist of letting surplus property and holding cash that is not required for trading operations.

Therefore care needs to be taken, particularly with the level of cash on the balance sheet, although the taxman will usually give advance clearance on the taper relief status of the company if so requested.

Taper Relief – Does it Protect You Against Inflation?

For long-term investors the introduction of taper relief has provided a generous tax break because in many ways it protects far more of your gains from the taxman than the old indexation allowance.

Unfortunately, however, it punishes short-term investors.

Example

Bobby invests £100,000 in shares for just under three years and earns a return of 8% per year. At the end of the period he will have a gain of £25,970 which will be fully taxed because he doesn't qualify for taper relief.

With inflation running at about 3% per year about £2,200 of the gain is purely inflationary – yet Bobby still has to pay tax on it.

However, the longer you hold on to your investments the more generous taper relief becomes. In many cases it provides *too much protection,* meaning that you will not have to pay tax on your profits after adjusting for inflation.

The optimum time period to hold on to your investments to maximise taper relief is 10 years because that is when the maximum 40% relief is obtained.

Example

Bobby holds on to his shares for 10 years. At the end of the period he will have earned a profit of £115,892. He qualifies for the maximum taper relief of 40%. This means £46,357 of his profits escape tax.

Now let's assume that the Bank of England has done its job right over the period and met its inflation target of 2%. What this means is that, of Bobby's total profits, 2% per year is purely inflationary.

Over 10 years this equates to £20,820 – the amount that would have been given as indexation relief under the old rules. However, Bobby's taper relief is far higher: £46,357. In effect the taxman has let him off having to pay tax on £25,537 of profits.

The Bank of England currently has an inflation target of 2%. Provided it meets this objective, long-term share investors will enjoy considerable tax benefits from the new taper relief system – profits that would have been taxed when indexation relief was around will now escape tax altogether.

Chapter 17

Tax Shelters: VCT and EIS Shares

A tax shelter is an investment that offers favourable tax treatment, either by allowing you to defer or avoid tax. They're often established by Governments to encourage funds to be invested in higher risk activities that wouldn't normally attract the average investor. The two best-known tax shelters for UK investors are:

- Enterprise Investment Scheme (EIS) shares.
- Venture Capital Trusts (VCTs).

Enterprise Investment Scheme (EIS) Shares

The EIS scheme offers two significant forms of tax relief: income tax relief and capital gains tax relief.

Income Tax

This allows an individual to obtain an income tax credit equal to 20% of the amount invested in EIS shares. The maximum investment that can be made is £200,000 for the 2005/2006 tax year. An income tax loss cannot be created, however.

Example

Johnny purchases qualifying EIS shares for £200,000. Assuming he has a tax liability from other income equal to £50,000, he will obtain income tax relief equal to £40,000 (£200,000 x 20%).

As a result he will only have to pay income tax of £10,000 (£50,000 less £40,000).

Capital Gains Tax

Enterprise Investment Schemes offer the following capital gains tax breaks:

- Capital gains from the sale of other assets (eg other shares or property) can be held over against qualifying EIS shares purchased up to one year prior to the disposal and three years after.
- Any capital gain arising when the EIS shares are sold is not taxable provided income tax relief has been given and not withdrawn and the shares are held for a qualifying period, which is usually three years.

Example
Peter makes a gain of £75,000 on a disposal of shares in Lucky plc, a major quoted company. As he is not an employee of the company he will not qualify for business asset taper relief and is concerned about his CGT exposure.

If he was to invest £75,000 in qualifying EIS shares within three years of making the sale capital gains tax will be deferred on the £75,000 until the earliest of the following:

- *The disposal of the EIS shares (excluding a disposal to a spouse)*
- *Peter ceases to be UK resident*
- *The company ceases to be a qualfying EIS company*

In addition the taxpayer can claim a lesser amount of relief. So, in the above example, if the disposal occurred in tax year 2005/2006 Peter could have claimed deferral relief of £66,500.

This would then leave a gain of £8,500 chargeable which, if no other gains existed during the tax year, would be fully offset by the annual exemption.

These reliefs sound very attractive. The problem is that they can be very restrictive and although a full analysis of the details of the EIS scheme is outside the scope of this book, it is important to note that EIS tax breaks only apply to 'qualifying' companies which essentially means that the company must be an unquoted trading company that falls within a list of approved trades.

Shares traded on the Alternative Investment Market are regarded as unquoted for this purpose and for the share speculator it is likely to only be AIM shares that have the potential to qualify under the EIS scheme.

If you are interested in exploring the opportunities available under the EIS scheme, it is important to obtain professional advice.

Venture Capital Trusts (VCTs)

Venture capital trusts were introduced to encourage individuals to invest in unquoted trading companies. Normally the VCT will be a quoted fund that invests in unquoted companies. VCTs offer a variety of generous tax breaks designed to offset the risks inherent in such companies:

- Dividends are completely tax free.
- Share subscribers (in other words, those who invest in the fund when it issues new shares) can obtain income tax relief equivalent to 40% of the the amount invested, up to a maximum of £200,000. This relief was increased in the 2004 Budget and applies for the 2004/2005 and 2005/2006 tax years only.
- There is no capital gains tax when you sell your VCT shares.
- The VCT itself does not pay corporation tax when it sells qualifying shares. This leaves more proceeds to distribute in the form of a tax-free dividend.

On the downside, in the 2004 Budget it was also announced that capital gains tax holdover relief ceased to apply on these investments from 5th April 2004.

It should be noted that the above tax breaks are only available to investors who subscribe for *new* VCT shares. If you buy existing shares through a stockbroker you are only entitled to the following tax breaks:

- Exemption from capital gains tax when you sell your shares.
- Tax-free dividends.

Income Tax Relief

For the 2004/2005 and 2005/2006 tax years subscribers to new VCT shares are entitled to 40% income tax relief on investments of up to £200,000 per year.

However, in order to prevent this relief being taken away, the shares must be retained for at least three years (five years if acquired before the 6th of April 2000).

It would be normal for the VCT to offer share subscribers a certificate of eligibility, including details of the share investment, and certifying that the shares and VCT are qualifying investments for the purpose of the tax reliefs.

Any claim for tax relief will be made on your self assessment return, although if an individual is expecting to obtain this relief, he can make a claim to reduce his payments on account for a tax year. Any underpayment will be charged interest between the relevant due dates.

In addition if an individual pays income tax via PAYE, he will be able to claim an adjustment to his tax code.

Example

Jack earns a £250,000 bonus during the 2005 tax year on which he expects to pay 40% tax amounting to £100,000.

To reduce the tax bill Jack subscribes for the maximum £200,000 of shares in a newly launched VCT.

He will be entitled to a tax credit equal to 40% x £200,000 = £80,000, thereby reducing tax on the bonus to just £20,000.

Note: If Jack's expected income tax liability was just £50,000, the £80,000 credit would reduce his income tax liability to nil, and would not create a repayment of income tax.

The Risks

In the above example Jack has generated an £80,000 tax saving but he ends up with £200,000 worth of venture capital trust shares which he has to hold on to for at least three years.

That may not be a bad thing: the shares might rocket in value... but they may also become almost worthless if the trust makes disastrous investment choices.

For example, if in three years' time the shares have fallen by more than 40%, Jack will be worse off than if he had just paid 40% tax on his bonus.

Nevertheless the income tax credit provides a massive cushion against any such fall and, with expert advice on which VCT to invest in, Jack could end up with a very profitable and tax-efficient investment.

Capital Gains Tax Relief

If Jack's shares have risen in value he will enjoy a further benefit: the gain will be completely tax free. Venture capital trust profits are exempt from capital gains tax.

In the same vein, however, no relief is available for capital losses.

The capital gains deferral provisions no longer apply, so you can no longer roll over capital gains from selling other shares or property investments and subscribe for new shares in a VCT.

The Inland Revenue has detailed rules that need to be satisified by a VCT in order for investors to qualify for the various tax breaks. It is not necessary to examine the rules here but it is important to be aware of them.

Chapter 18

Equities vs Property for Tax Savings

Your decision to invest in equities or property will probably be based mainly on non-tax factors – primarily how much you expect shares and house prices to rise in the months and years ahead.

Risk is another important consideration. Many investors regard shares as high risk and property as a much safer alternative, especially after the bursting of the dot com bubble in 2000 and the bear market that followed.

As it happens, many property investors expose themselves to even greater levels of risk than stock market investors because of the large borrowings they shoulder.

Whereas shares can be bought with relatively small sums of money, very few investors can buy a property outright. As a result many investors are exposed to the perils of having insufficient rental income to cover their mortgage repayments.

As with everything, a sense of balance is important and most investors would probably be well advised to consider investing in both equities and property.

While non-tax factors are the most important, there are some very important differences between the way shares and property are taxed.

The main differences can be summarised as follows:

- **Income tax.** Share dividends are taxed at either an effective 0% or 25% (if you are a higher rate taxpayer); property rentals are usually taxed at 22% or 40%.

- **Stamp duty.** Share investors pay stamp duty at a flat rate of 0.5%. Property investors can end up paying zero per cent but as much as 4%.

- **Annual CGT allowance.** By selling off small parcels of shares each year share investors can make use of their annual capital gains tax allowance much more readily than property investors.

- **Special reliefs.** Property investors benefit from a number of generous capital gains tax reliefs when they sell a property that was previously their main residence.

- **ISAs.** Income and capital gains from shares and other financial assets can be protected from the taxman by using an ISA wrapper. Property investments do not qualify.

- **Tax deductions.** Property investors can more readily gear their investments by borrowing money and offsetting interest charges against their rental income. Although risky it is regarded by many as the key to real estate riches.

Let's examine some of these differences in more detail.

Income Tax

Rental income is generally taxed much more heavily than dividend income. As an extreme example, if you earned all your income from shares you would not pay a penny in tax, provided your total income was less than £37,295. If you earned £37,295 in property rental profits you would pay over £6,500 in tax. Higher rate taxpayers only pay 25% tax on their dividends, compared with 40% on their rents.

Should this have any bearing on your investment decisions? In some respects, yes. For example, if you're investing for income and comparing yields on different types of assets it's worth remembering that 8% from property is no better than 6.4% from shares if you are a higher rate taxpayer. Similarly, 7% from property is the same as 5.6% from shares and 6% from property is no better than 4.8% from shares!

Stamp Duty

Property stamp duty (known as stamp duty land tax) has risen dramatically in recent years. The current rates are as follows:

Purchases not exceeding £120,000	Nil
Purchases between £120,000 and £250,000	1%
Purchases between £250,000 and £500,000	3%
Purchases over £500,000	4%

While these rates are far higher than the 0.5% on shares, a large number of property investors will be paying no more than 1%, especially those investing in flats in regions other than the South East.

Furthermore, share portfolios are more likely to be 'churned' than property portfolios, leading to multiple stamp duty charges over time. Nevertheless it would be fair to say that, taking into account all purchase costs, including legal fees, property transaction costs are far higher than those applicable to shares and other financial assets. Over a longish period of time, as the property rises in value, these extra costs are likely to be insignificant.

Annual CGT Exemption

Such is the importance of the annual capital gains tax allowance that we've devoted a whole chapter to it (see Chapter 9). For a married couple it's worth £6,800 per year in saved tax (£8,500 x 2 X 40%). Over a ten-year period that's a tax saving of £68,000! Both property investors and share investors qualify for the allowance but, in reality, property investors get to use it very rarely, as most would find it almost impossible to sell property every year. Share investors are much better placed to exploit the allowance by making annual share disposals.

But is this necessarily a sensible strategy? To find out let's take a look at a detailed example.

Example

Mr and Mrs Peterson invest £250,000 in a property, Mr and Mrs Smith invest £250,000 in a FTSE tracker fund. Both couples earn 8% per year over a 15-year period.

To make the most of their annual capital gains tax exemptions the Smiths sell some investment fund units each year and reinvest immediately in a ***different*** *index tracker (to avoid the 'bed and breakfasting' regulations – see Chapter 4).*

We'll assume that the Smiths sell just enough units to make full use of their CGT exemptions and that the allowance increases by £300 per year. We'll also ignore all income and transaction costs.

After 15 years the Petersons decide to sell their property which is now worth £793,042 – a profit of £543,042. To calculate their tax bill we deduct £217,217 taper relief (40% x £543,042) and their annual CGT exemptions. We assume the exemption is now worth £12,700 (£25,400 for a married couple). The Petersons' total tax bill will be:

£543,042 - £217,217 - £25,400 x 40% tax = £120,170

This leaves the Petersons with £672,872 after tax.

What about Mr and Mrs Smith, the share investors? Their pre-tax returns are identical to the Petersons – after 15 years their portfolio is worth £793,042. However, the tax calculation is a little more complex. Remember, each year they've been selling just enough units to make use of their CGT exemptions and investing these tax-free amounts in new index tracker funds.

After 15 years, they therefore hold investments in 15 funds. When they sell, each fund will qualify for a different amount of taper relief because each fund has been held for a different length of time. For example, the fund invested in after year one qualifies for the full 40% taper relief because it has been held for more than 10 years. But the fund they invested in at the end of year 14 does not enjoy any taper relief.

Taking all this into account, the Smiths end up with £696,301 after tax – £23,429 more than the Petersons.

This is an intriguing result... but for all the wrong reasons!

Although the Smiths have an extra £23,429, which no investor would sniff at, this is only 3% more money than the Petersons. And it took 15 years to earn!

So to answer the question: "Should the fact that share investors can readily exploit their annual CGT allowance influence the decision to buy shares or property?", the answer is definitely NO.

No sane investor would ditch one asset class in favour of another to earn a measly extra 3% after 15 years.

So why is the difference not more extreme? After all, the Petersons got to use only one year's worth of capital gains tax allowances whereas the Smiths got to use 15 years' worth of allowances.

The answer lies with taper relief. The Smiths make more regular use of their annual exemption by selling units but lose out on taper relief because many of their subsequent investment fund purchases have been held for less than 10 years. The Petersons only qualify for one year's annual exemption but the maximum 40% taper relief because their one and only investment, the property, has been held for more than 10 years.

In total the Petersons can claim £217,217 of taper relief, compared with only £149,425 by the Smiths.

There is clearly an important trade-off between making maximum use of your CGT exemption and maximum use of taper relief . Every time you sell an asset to exploit your CGT exemption the taper relief 'clock' is reset to zero.

Wider Implications for Share Investment

The above example has a wider interpretation. For example, it could be used to compare two stock market investors, one buying and holding, the other making frequent disposals.

Many stock market investors believe they should sell shares as often as possible to take advantage of their annual CGT exemptions. However, from a tax perspective the trade off is between making frequent use of your annual allowance and losing out on taper relief on your new investments.

Selling shares results in transaction costs and you also have to watch out for the share matching rules (see Chapter 4). Although you may save some tax in the long run, you may also be substituting good investments with poor ones as a result.

Capital Gains Tax Reliefs

If you sell a property that was previously your main residence, a portion of the capital gain is tax free. The tax-free portion is calculated as follows:

Capital gain x Period of occupation/Period of ownership

This is what's known as the Principal Private Residence Relief (PPR). That's not the interesting part, however. There is an extra concession that could save you a small fortune in capital gains tax. What it says is that the last 36 months of your ownership of the property are deemed to be a period of private occupation, *irrespective of whether you actually lived in the property during that period.*

In other words, you can move out of your home, rent it out for three years, and not pay a penny in capital gains tax.

If you hold on to the property for more than three years capital gains tax will again come into play. However, if you're renting out the property you will also qualify for something called Private Letting Relief. This is calculated as the *lowest* of the following:

- The amount of PPR relief you're entitled to when you sell, or
- The gain arising during the letting period, or
- £40,000.

No private letting relief will be given unless the property has been your only or main residence. However, there is no need for the property to be occupied *after* the letting period to obtain this relief. The critical point is that this quirk in the tax law could affect your decision to invest in property versus shares. Whereas most investment decisions are based on non-tax factors, this is an example where tax may be the most important factor.

Example

Stuart purchases a small residence in Essex in 2001 for £200,000. A year later he inherits another property in Docklands and decides to live in that one instead (it's much closer to his job as a fund manager in Canary Wharf). He now has two choices: hold on to the Essex property and let it out, or sell it and invest the proceeds in shares. To keep things simple we'll assume each investment grows by 15% per year and could be sold for £400,000 in 2005. We'll also ignore all transaction costs. (It doesn't really matter if you think these assumptions are unrealistic – it's the tax angle that matters most here.)

Property

If Stuart holds on to the Essex property his profit after five years is £200,000. The taxable gain will be reduced by the following reliefs:

- *Principal Private Residence Relief = £160,000 (£200,000 x 4 years/5 years)*
- *Private Letting Relief = £40,000*

Remember the PPR relief is calculated over four years: one year of occupation and three years of 'deemed occupation'. Stuart's total reliefs come to £200,000, wiping out the capital gain for tax purposes. Taper relief and the annual CGT allowance don't even come into the picture.

Stuart is left with capital of £400,000 to do with as he pleases.

Shares

What if he decided to invest in shares instead? He sells the Essex property after year one for £230,000 and invests this tax-free lump sum. Four years later the share portfolio is worth £400,000. What's the likely tax bill?

Profit	*£170,000*
Less:	
Taper relief @10%	*£17,000*
CGT allowance	*£8,500*
Gain	*£144,500*
Tax @ 40%	*£57,800*

Stuart would pay no tax on the property but £57,800 if he invested in shares. The property investment profits are £170,000; the share investment profits are just £112,200 – remember pre-tax returns were identical!

In summary, there are very few medium-term investments that are more tax efficient than a former residence. You can hold on to it for three years and not pay a penny in capital gains tax. Further tax breaks are available if the property is let out for a further period.

Other Types of Shares & Property

So far we've only compared residential property and quoted shares. However, a lot of commercial property and 'unquoted' shares, including AIM-listed shares, qualify for the more generous 'business-asset' taper relief. Business taper exempts 50% of your profits from tax after just one year and 75% after just two years!

(Most commercial property let to *unquoted* trading companies has qualified for business asset taper relief since 6 April 2000 – for more information see our guide *How to Avoid Property Tax*.)

We compare business and non-business taper relief more in Chapter 16. However, when comparing the tax treatment of property and shares it's also important to understand how business taper relief could affect your decisions.

Example

Petra has the opportunity to invest in one of the following:

- *A two-bedroom flat.*
- *1,000 shares in BIG plc, a FTSE 100 company.*
- *100,000 shares in Internet Sales Ltd, an AIM listed company.*
- *An industrial unit intended to be let to an unquoted trading company.*

Petra's total initial investment is £100,000, and for the sake of simplicity let's assume each investment will show total growth of 10% per year.

Ignoring the annual capital gains tax exemption, the taxable gains after various time periods would be as follows:

Yrs	***Flat***	***BIG***	***Internet***	***Industrial***
1	*£10,000*	*£10,000*	*£5,000*	*£5,000*
2	*£21,000*	*£21,000*	*£5,250*	*£5,250*
3	*£31,445*	*£31,445*	*£8,275*	*£8,275*
4	*£41,769*	*£41,769*	*£11,603*	*£11,603*
5	*£51,893*	*£51,893*	*£15,263*	*£15,263*

The taxable gains arising on the business assets (the internet company and the commercial property) are substantially lower than those arising on the non-business assets (the quoted shares and the investment property). This means the after-tax profits on the business assets are significantly higher.

Hence you have to be careful about not only the *type* of asset you are comparing, e.g. shares versus property, but the *sector/market* as well. A 30% return after two years from an AIM listed company could dwarf a 30% return from residential property, after tax has been taken into consideration.

Remember too that dividends are often taxed at a much lower rate than rental income (either 0% or 25% compared with 22% or 40%), and therefore the dividend/rental yield will be a key factor in certain cases.

Chapter 19

Non-Resident and Offshore Tax Planning

Becoming non-resident is of great interest to many people who wish to avoid UK taxes. However, it's worth noting that tax rates in most industrialised countries are *higher* than those in the UK.

Therefore if you emigrate to avoid tax, you may end up jumping out of the frying pan and into the fire!

To achieve a permanent reduction in tax it is necessary to move to a tax haven or low-tax jurisdiction such as Jersey or the Isle of Man.

In this chapter we'll conduct a broad overview of non-residence tax issues. More in-depth information is contained in the Taxcafe.co.uk guide *Non-Resident & Offshore Tax Planning*.

In the sections that follow we'll take a look at Inland Revenue's rules regarding residence and domicile and examine how the three most important taxes (namely, income tax, capital gains and inheritance tax) are affected by a change in your status.

Residence

There is no formal legal definition of 'residence'. Inland Revenue's practice - based on a mixture of statute and court decisions - is to regard you as resident in the UK during a tax year if :

- You spend 183 days or more in the UK during the tax year, or
- Although here for less than 183 days, you have spent more than 90 days per year in the country over the past four years (taken as an average). You will then be classed as UK resident from the fifth year.

These rules have no statutory force and should be regarded as guidance only. For example, an individual who regularly returns to the UK for 87 days per tax year may still be regarded as UK resident.

A person can also be resident in two countries at the same time. It is therefore not possible to escape UK residence by arguing that you are resident elsewhere.

It is important to note that UK residence is a question of fact and not intention. Therefore although an individual may intend to leave before the 183-day limit, if he is forced to remain in the UK as a result of exceptional circumstances he will nevertheless be regarded as UK resident.

Ordinary Residence

Even if you qualify as non-resident you may still fall into the taxman's clutches by being classified as *UK ordinary resident.*

There is also no statutory test of ordinary residence. You will be classified as a UK ordinary resident if the UK is your normal place of residence.

On leaving the country you will continue to be regarded as UK ordinary resident unless you go abroad with the intention of taking up permanent residence overseas. Inland Revenue normally interprets 'permanent' to mean three years or more.

It is therefore possible to be non-UK resident but UK ordinary resident. This would occur, for example, if you go abroad for a long holiday and do not return to the UK during a particular tax year. You will continue to be classed as UK ordinary resident until you can show that you have taken up a permanent residence elsewhere.

The consequence of being classed as a UK ordinary resident is that you will have to pay UK capital gains tax on your worldwide gains.

A person who is UK resident under the 183-day test may not necessarily be UK ordinary resident. He will then have to pay tax on overseas income/gains to the extent that the income/proceeds are brought into the UK (this applies to Commonwealth and Irish citizens).

However, a person who is UK resident as a result of the 90-day test would find it difficult to argue that he or she is not also UK ordinary resident and therefore worldwide income and gains would be taxed as they arise.

One factor that is likely to be taken into account in assessing ordinary residence is whether you continue to own and occupy property in the UK. In particular, where the use or occupation of the property is combined with other factors, such as regular visits to the UK only slightly below the 90-day average. This will be persuasive evidence that you have not taken up a permanent residence elsewhere.

However, subject to this, a person who leaves the UK will cease to be UK ordinary resident if he/she establishes non-UK residence for three consecutive tax years.

Summary

As you can see, residence issues can be fairly complex. It is useful to consolidate the above:

- Individuals who are UK resident/ordinarily resident and domiciled will be liable to UK tax on their worldwide income and gains
- Individuals who are UK resident/ordinarily resident but non-UK domiciled will be liable to UK tax on overseas income/gains to the extent that the income/proceeds are remitted to the UK.
- An individual who is UK resident, but not ordinarily resident, will also be subject to the remittance basis for overseas income and gains (provided they are a Commonwealth or Irish citizen)

- An individual who is non-resident and not ordinarily resident will be liable to UK income tax on UK source income and will be exempt from UK capital gains tax on all assets (whether situated in the UK or overseas) except for assets used in a UK trade.

Domicile

The concept of 'domicile' is extremely important when it comes to both inheritance tax and overseas tax planning.

Losing your UK domicile is substantially more difficult than losing your UK resident status. A person is normally domiciled in the country that he regards as his home, not the place where he happens to be temporarily living.

It is, in a sense, the country that you regard as your true 'homeland' and has frequently been described as the country in which a person intends to die.

It is therefore possible for a person to live abroad for 40 years yet still remain legally domiciled in the UK.

While it is possible to be resident in two countries at the same time, it is only possible to be domiciled in one.

There are three types of domicile:

Domicile of Origin

A domicile of origin is acquired when a person is born. Under normal circumstances this is the father's domicile at the date of the child's birth. If the parents are unmarried, it is the mother's domicile.

A domicile of origin continues unless the individual acquires either a domicile of dependency or a domicile of choice (see below). This new domicile will remain in force unless it is abandoned, in which case the domicile of origin is revived.

Domicile of Choice

In order to acquire a domicle of choice a person must voluntarily make a new territory his residence and intend to remain there for the rest of his days – unless and until something occurs to make him change his mind.

Obtaining a domicile of choice is primarily a question of intent. However, once such a domicile has been established it is relatively difficult to abandon. It would be necessary for an individual to cease to reside in the country of choice indefinitely.

Domicile of Dependency

This type of domicile only applies to children under the age of 16. A child's domicile of origin is replaced by a domicile of dependency if there is a change in the father's domicile (mother's domicile in the case of unmarried couples). If this happens, the parent's domicile of choice becomes the child's domicile of dependency. The child keeps this domicile unless he does not live in the territory and never intends to live there. In this case the child's domicile of origin revives.

Example

John was born in Latvia and would therefore ordinarily be regarded as being of Latvian domicile. John went to live in France and successfully established France as his domicile of choice. His son, Jack, who was born in Latvia, would also have a Latvian domicile of origin, however, he would 'inherit' his father's French domicile. This would be his domicile of dependency.

If Jack intends to permanently return to Latvia on his 18th birthday and makes preparations for this, his domicile would revert to his domicile of origin. The domicile of dependency has essentially been changed as by indicating his intention to return to Latvia, the domicile of origin 'reasserts' itself.

Income Tax

Income tax is based primarily on residence. If you are resident in the UK, you are normally liable to UK tax on your worldwide income. If you are not UK resident you are still liable to UK tax on income arising in the UK, but your non-UK income is outside the scope of UK income tax.

The terms of any double taxation agreement between the UK and your country of residence also need to be considered.

If you are UK resident but non-UK domiciled, you will only be liable to UK income tax on your overseas income if you remit the proceeds to the UK.

Therefore any dividends from an overseas company would not be taxed if they were paid into an overseas bank account.

Capital Gains Tax (CGT)

Capital gains tax depends on both residence and *ordinary residence*. If you cease to be resident in the UK without also ceasing to be ordinarily resident here, you will remain subject to UK capital gains tax in respect of any gains made on your worldwide assets.

If you cease to be both resident and ordinarily resident, you are outside the scope of UK capital gains tax, even on UK assets.

There are, however, tax anti-avoidance rules that state that in order for an individual to avoid capital gains tax it is usually necessary to remain non-resident for **five complete tax years**.

Any gains on assets disposed of during the period of non-residence would then escape UK capital gains tax completely.

It should be noted that this rule only applies where the individual has been UK resident for at least four of the seven tax years prior to the year of departure.

If you have not been UK resident for this period it is possible to avoid capital gains tax by becoming non-UK resident AND non-UK ordinarily resident for the tax year in which the disposal takes place.

Assuming this is not the case, and you are subject to the five-year rule, no assessment is made unless you return to the UK within the five-year period. Provided you remain non-resident for at least five complete tax years, gains realised during the first five complete tax years of non-residence are tax free.

If you become UK resident within the five tax years limit, any gains on assets sold during your absence from the UK will be assessed in the tax year you return as gains of that year.

Example

Peter has decided to sell his shares in Kick plc during the 2005/2006 tax year. Assuming he has satisfied the Inland Revenue as to his non-residence status, he will be non-resident during this tax year and any disposal of his shares will be ***initially*** *free from UK capital gains tax.*

Provided he now remains non-resident for five complete tax years, in other words until at least 6 April 2010, there will be no tax to pay.

If he returns to the UK before this date he will become liable to UK capital gains tax, as if the gain arose in the tax year of his return.

Non-UK Domiciliaries

Individuals who are not of UK domicile, even though UK resident, are subject to special rules on overseas asset sales.

Gains on disposals of overseas assets are only subject to UK capital gains tax if the proceeds are brought into the UK.

Example

Jack, of Jamaican domicile, has been UK resident for five years. He has recently disposed of £100,000 worth of shares in a non-UK company, showing a profit of £10,000.

If Jack brings all the proceeds into the UK, the full £10,000 will be taxed (subject to any applicable reliefs).

If Jack remitted £50,000 into the UK, half of the gain (£5,000) would be taxed, again subject to any available reliefs.

Inheritance Tax (IHT)

Inheritance tax is based on domicile. If a person is domiciled in the UK he is liable to UK inheritance tax on his *worldwide* assets, even though he may be both resident and ordinarily resident in another country. If a person is not domiciled here, he is generally liable to inheritance tax on his UK assets only.

Therefore a non-UK domiciliary is still liable to UK inheritance on any UK shareholdings he may own.

In addition to the general rules regarding domicile, there are also deemed domicile rules for inheritance tax purposes. These apply to deem you to be UK domiciled for inheritance tax purposes where:

- You have been resident in the UK for 17 out of the last 20 years.
- You have lost your UK residence in the last three years.

TAX-PLANNING OPPORTUNITIES

Capital and Income Accounts

It is generally advisable for non-domiciliaries to have separate bank accounts to separate their overseas income (taxable when brought into the UK) from their capital (tax free when brought into the UK). Failure to do this may result in Inland Revenue deeming the amounts remitted to the UK to be taxable interest.

Furthermore the proceeds of any foreign gains realized *prior* to obtaining UK residence should be kept in a separate account, along with any gifts or inherited money. Income can then be remitted from this fund free of UK tax.

Also, the proceeds of overseas gains realized whilst UK resident should be kept in a separate account. These funds will be subject to capital gains tax when remitted to the UK, yet it would be possible to remit proceeds with relatively small gains in stages so as to utilize the capital gains tax annual exemption (in other words, remit £8,500 worth of gains during the 2005/2006 tax year).

Offshore Bonds

Offshore bonds offer opportunities for individuals expecting to be non-resident or have a lower income on the date of encashment.

By choosing an investment that benefits from 'gross roll up', no income will be taxed during the life of the bond.

It's only when encashment takes place that income tax is payable. However, by arranging to be non-resident any UK income tax will be eliminated, although clearly any overseas taxation consequences would have to be considered.

Time Apportionment

Time apportionment is a relief which investors in offshore bonds receive for the time they are not resident in the UK and is particularly beneficial for returning expatriates. As an example, if you spend half the investment period outside the UK as a non-resident, then any tax liability will be calculated depending on the proportion of time actually resident in the UK.

Therefore any expatriates who suspect that they may return to the UK, should consider owning an offshore bond for the potential tax-planning benefits available under the time apportionment rules.

Example

Percy takes out a £10,000 bond while living abroad. This increases to £20,000 over the next five years. He then moves back to the UK and decides to top the bond up by a further £80,000 (total investment £100,000). Over the next five years the fund value grows to £200,000, at which point Percy decides to cash it in. The total gain is therefore £110,000, of which £100,000 has occurred within the past five years.

Time apportionment applies because although the total ownership is 10 years, five years was spent as a non-resident and, as such, the chargeable gain is reduced to £55,000.

Summary

There are opportunities available to non-UK resident individuals to dispose of UK shareholdings free of UK capital gains tax.

Note that the position for share traders is more complex. Share traders will be subject to UK income tax on their UK source income and, as such, a non-resident individual trading in the UK would have UK income, which would be subject to UK income tax.

Share traders, will therefore be subject to UK income tax on any profits arising from their UK share dealing trade.

Chapter 20

Making the Most of Gilts and Corporate Bonds

When Governments or big companies wish to borrow money they issue bonds. These 'chunks of debt' will pay you interest at a fixed rate for a number of years, typically five to 20 years. Bonds, especially government bonds, are potentially 'risk-free' investments because they guarantee to repay your initial capital at the end of the borrowing period.

Although the borrower guarantees to repay your initial capital at the end of the bond's life, bonds can be bought or sold on the open market at any time before that. The price of a bond during its lifetime is determined by the market level of interest rates. When interest rates go up bond prices fall, when interest rates go down, bond prices rise.

Hence bond returns can come in two forms: interest *and* capital growth. All bond investors earn interest but only those who invest during a period of falling interest rates enjoy capital growth.

There are several reasons investors buy bonds. Most investment experts would argue that a well-balanced growth portfolio contains a mix of equities, property, bonds and cash. Younger investors, or those with a greater appetite for risk, are usually encouraged to put most of their money into high-growth assets like equities. Older and more cautious investors are encouraged to hold a greater proportion of less risky assets like bonds.

There are several ways you can invest in bonds. You can either buy them directly through your stockbroker, just like most share investments. Or you can invest indirectly through a unit trust.

For example, high-yielding corporate bond funds became extremely popular as the level of interest rates fell during the late

1990s and investors looked for ways of boosting their returns. You can also invest in bonds via a private pension plan or ISA.

The reason we mention all this is because, depending on *why* and *how* you invest in bonds, tax can have a massive impact on the outcome. The way bonds are taxed makes them extremely attractive to some types of investor and extremely unattractive to others.

Before we explore this issue further it's essential to understand exactly how bond returns are taxed.

How Are Bonds Taxed?

The answer depends on whether you invest in UK or overseas bonds or corporate bonds and whether you invest directly or indirectly:

- **UK Government bonds (also known as 'gilts').** Interest income is fully taxed at either the 'savings rate' of 20% or the higher income rate of 40%. Capital gains are completely tax free.

- **UK Corporate bonds.** Interest income is fully taxed at either 20% or 40%. Capital gains are tax free, provided the bond satisfies various Inland Revenue conditions (see below).

- **Overseas bonds.** Here we're talking about non-UK bonds, such as US Treasuries. Interest income is fully taxed at either 20% or 40%. Capital gains are subject to capital gains tax.

- **Bond funds.** There are many unit trusts (or OEICs) that invest solely in bonds. You can invest in both UK and international bond funds and ones that focus on government or corporate bonds. If you invest directly (rather than through an ISA) interest income is fully taxed at either 20% or 40%. Furthermore, capital gains are subject to capital gains tax, even if the fund only invests in otherwise exempt UK Government and corporate bonds.

- **Bond ISAs and Pensions.** Many bond funds come with their own ISA 'wrappers'. In this case all income and capital gains are tax free. You can also invest in bonds through a private pension plan, such as a stakeholder pension. Most investment companies will let you choose a portfolio with a heavy weighting of bonds. All income and capital gains are tax free.

Clearly *how* you invest (directly or via a unit trust, pension plan or ISA) and *where* you invest (in UK or overseas bonds) could have an enormous impact on how your capital gains are taxed. The investor who makes significant capital gains from UK gilts will end up much better off than the investor who earns similar capital gains from US Treasuries. The investor who makes significant capital gains from UK gilts will end up much better off than the investor who makes significant capital gains from a UK gilt unit trust.

As we keep emphasizing, tax is not the only consideration. For example, it may be that by investing through a fund you will enjoy significantly higher capital gains than you would by investing directly. (In other words, the fund manager may be a better investor than you are!) In such cases, the after-tax returns from the unit trust could still be significantly higher.

What about interest income? With the exception of ISAs and pensions, in all cases income is fully taxable – it doesn't matter if you invest in UK or overseas bonds, directly or through a unit trust.

So where does all this leave the investor trying to allocate his funds between equities and bonds?

Equities vs Bonds

Let's say you're a long-term investor accumulating capital over a number of years by reinvesting the returns from your equities and bonds. Most long-term bond investors are looking mainly for interest income because it is very difficult to guarantee long-term capital growth from bonds. There are two questions this investor needs to answer: "How much should I invest in bonds as part of my long-term investment strategy and how should I invest?"

There have been numerous studies comparing equity and bond returns over long periods of time. This research makes fascinating reading but very little of it looks at how *tax* affects overall returns. To some extent this is understandable because there is no 'one-size-fits-all' tax rate that applies to every investor. However, in many cases tax completely alters the outcome so it is essential for any investor wishing to hold bonds to look at after-tax returns.

Example – Bonds versus Equities, the extreme case

Mr and Mrs Edwards inherit £25,000 and decide to invest the entire amount in equities for 20 years to provide a retirement nest egg. They earn a return of 5% per year, all of which comes in the form of capital growth rather than income.

Mr and Mrs Brown also inherit £25,000 but, being risk averse, decide to invest all their money in bonds, earning 5% interest per year. They also invest for 20 years and reinvest all their income. We'll also assume they make no capital gains or losses over this period, which is akin to investing in a new bond issue and holding it until maturity date.

Of course, it's rather unkind of us to assume that Mr and Mrs Edwards will earn the same return as the Browns. Because equities are more volatile than bonds, investors expect them to deliver a higher return – the so-called 'equity risk premium' – over the long run. However, to make useful after-tax comparisons it makes sense to assume that returns are identical.

If we ignore tax then both couples end up with identical sums of money after 20 years – £66,332 each. However, if we compare *after-tax* returns the picture is completely different. The share investors pay no tax from year to year, only when they sell up at the end of the period. Furthermore, when they eventually sell, the amount taxed will be reduced by 40% taper relief and two annual CGT exemptions. The result is they don't pay any capital gains tax on their profits and end up with the whole £66,332 after 20 years.

The bond investors are not so lucky. They pay income tax *every* year on *all* of their interest income. Assuming they're in the top tax bracket, we find that Mr and Mrs Brown end up with just £45,153.

In other words, the share investors end up with 47% more money than the bond investors, despite earning identical pre-tax returns!

Why do the equity investors fare so much better? The obvious reason is that Mr and Mrs Edwards can claim 40% taper relief and their gain is reduced by the annual CGT exemption. However, there is also a more subtle explanation.

Share investors only pay CGT when they *sell* an asset, not from year to year. Until this time they have full use of the taxman's money to generate further capital gains. Bond investors have to pay tax every year on their interest income and therefore have fewer funds left to reinvest each year.

For example, let's assume that, like the bond investors, the Edwards pay 40% tax on *all* their equity profits – there is no taper relief and no annual exemption.

The only difference is the Edwards pay tax only at the end of the investment period. In this case the equity investors would still end up with about 10% more capital than the bond investors!

This interesting result can be put down solely to the fact that the equity investors only pay tax at the end of the period rather than from year to year.

In other words, deferring tax by investing in assets whose returns can be 'rolled up' before tax is payable can boost returns significantly.

The Inflation Danger

Mr and Mrs Brown, the bond investors in the above example, may be perfectly happy earning a lower return than Mr and Mrs Edwards, the equity investors. After all, their investment carries significantly less risk. However, by avoiding one risk they may be exposing themselves to another: inflation.

At present anyone earning interest is heavily penalised by the way the UK tax system fails to distinguish between 'nominal' and 'real' interest rates. The nominal interest rate is what the bond pays you. The real interest rate is the nominal interest rate less the rate of inflation. The real interest rate represents the actual or *real* increase in your wealth.

Say you earn 4.5% interest and the inflation rate is 3%. Your real interest rate is 1.5%. If the tax system was fair you would only have to pay tax on this portion of your returns.

Unfortunately, however, it is not! Because tax is payable on the whole 4%, there's a good chance that your investment will not keep up with inflation, making you a bit poorer with every year that passes.

For example, subtracting tax at 40% leaves you with an interest rate of just 2.7% which is less than some measures of the inflation rate. Even if you only pay tax at 20% you will only end up with 3.2%, just higher than certain measures of inflation.

This is the problem faced by the long-term saver trying to accumulate wealth by investing in bonds. Even if he invests in high-yielding corporate bonds, it is very unlikely that he will earn anything more than a modest real return on his money – at most about 1% per year.

For this reason, direct investment in gilts and corporate bonds is not a viable investment for anyone trying to accumulate wealth. Bonds are only attractive if you manage to earn some capital growth as well, for example by investing in an actively managed bond fund.

However, the fees (often 4% upfront and 1% per year thereafter) and tax (remember capital gains from bond funds are taxable) may absorb much of the benefit. And if you're unlucky you may even lose money if the fund manager gets it wrong.

In many ways the 'halcyon days' for bond investors are over. Long-term interest rates have fallen dramatically over the last couple of decades due to big structural changes in developed country economies that have seen inflation rates and interest rates fall dramatically. Such spectacular returns will probably not be seen again for many years.

There is only one way to invest in bonds if you want to earn a real return on your money: using ISAs and private pensions.

ISAs and Personal Pensions

If you don't want to invest all your savings in equities and want at least a portion of your assets held in less risky assets like bonds, the only way to earn an attractive after-tax return is to invest in a tax-sheltered product such as an ISA or personal pension. In this case all your interest earnings are tax free and it is likely that you will earn a return high enough to beat inflation and grow your capital steadily over time.

For example, if Mr and Mrs Brown, the bond investors in the above example, had sheltered their money in an ISA, instead of investing directly in bonds, they would have ended up with £66,332 instead of just £45,153.

In fact, it could be argued that cautious investors who want to put some of their savings into low-risk investments should use ALL of their ISA allowances to invest in bonds. After all, interest from bonds and bank accounts is heavily taxed whereas share profits are taxed more leniently, so it makes sense to use your ISA allowance in a way that gets you more 'bang for your buck'.

This would certainly be the case if you expected to earn *identical* returns from your bonds and shares. But what if, to make things more realistic, you expect your shares to do better than your bonds over time? In this case your share profits, though taxed at a lower rate, will be significantly higher resulting in a higher tax bill. So you may still save more tax by using your ISA allowance to invest in shares, even though they are taxed at a lower rate.

It all depends on how much better your shares perform, how long you invest and what you do with the money at the end of the day.

Chapter 21

How to Avoid Income Tax on Your Dividends

Investors can put their money into all sorts of income-generating assets, the most obvious ones being shares for dividends, property for rents, and bonds and cash for interest.

Each has benefits and drawbacks. There is no risk investing in Government bonds and very little risk investing in bank deposits. However, as shown in the previous chapter, these investments offer little or no protection against inflation.

Property rents rise over time but your income could suffer if the property is empty for a protracted period or if you incur unexpectedly high costs associated with the property.

Share dividends also offer protection against inflation but dividends can be cut or fall away completely if the company experiences financial hardship or goes bust. This risk can, however, be reduced by investing in an income unit trust or other income-focused investment fund.

One of the prime considerations for income investors is how big the *yield* is on different types of assets. By yield we simply mean income expressed as a percentage of the amount invested. A £100 asset that pays £10 has a 10% yield. Care has to be exercised when comparing yields on different investments because of factors such as tax, hidden costs and inflation protection.

Many investors are lured by high *initial* yields. For example, a corporate bond yielding 5% appears a lot more attractive than a share paying 3%. However, some assets, in particular shares, generally offer low initial yields but the prospect of a steadily rising income to protect you against inflation. Bank deposits and bonds, with the exception of index-linked gilts, offer no such protection and you're likely to see the real value of your income erode over time.

Caution also has to be exercised when comparing income yields on different types of investment as there is often a wide divergence between *gross* income yields and *net* income yields. By 'gross' we mean income before deducting all costs and tax.

For example, if you buy a property with a rental yield of 8% there's a good chance that well over half of this will be eaten up by tax and other costs... even if you buy the property outright without using borrowed money. From the property's rental income you have to deduct maintenance costs and wear and tear, insurance and letting agent's fees and it's not uncommon for property to lie vacant for one month out of every 12.

With shares there are no hidden costs to worry about – what you see is what you get! So a dividend yield of 7% from shares is far more attractive than a rental yield of 7%.

Furthermore, dividends are taxed much more favourably than most other types of income. Higher-rate taxpayers only have to pay 25% tax on their dividends, compared with 40% on their rental profits and 40% on their interest income. So even if your property and shares pay you the same income, the taxman will let you keep 15% more of your share income.

And if you're a basic-rate taxpayer you don't have to pay any tax on your dividends, whereas you have to pay 22% tax on your rental profits and 20% on your interest income. A married couple, who earn no other income, can therefore each receive dividend cheques of about £37,000 without paying a penny in income tax!

Another important difference between dividends and property rents is that for higher-rate taxpayers dividends can be converted into completely tax-free income by investing through an ISA. Basic-rate taxpayers receive no tax benefits from ISA dividends.

The tax treatment of dividends can be extremely confusing because of terms like 'tax credit', 'net dividend' and 'gross dividend'. In reality it's quite simple when you cut through all the jargon. In this chapter we will explain in plain English how dividends are taxed. Then we'll look at some useful tax-avoidance strategies.

DEFINITIONS

Net Dividend

This is the most important dividend number because it is the actual payment you receive from the company whose shares you own. In other words, the cheque you receive is the net dividend. If you are a higher-rate taxpayer (see Appendix A) you will then have to pay income tax of 25% on this amount. Other taxpayers pay no further tax on their dividends.

Gross Dividend

This is calculated by 'grossing up your net dividend'. To do this you multiply the net dividend by 10/9. For example, if your net dividend is £100, the gross dividend is:

£100 x 100/90 = £111.11

This amount is then used when calculating your annual tax bill, as will be shown below.

Tax Credit

When you receive your dividend cheque (your net dividend) it will also detail an amount of 'tax credit'. This is simply 10% of your gross dividend. So if the net dividend is £100 and the gross dividend is £111.11, the dividend tax credit is:

£111.11 x 10% = £11.11

It is important to note that the tax credit cannot be used to create an income tax refund.

Are Gross Dividends and Tax Credits Important?

It's the net dividend that is the most important number for your financial planning because this is the actual income you receive. Gross dividends and tax credits are only important when it comes to doing your paperwork and filling in your tax return.

The Dividend Tax Calculation

Although the 'effective' tax rate for dividends is 25% for higher-rate taxpayers and 0% for other taxpayers, the 'formal' tax rates are 32.5% and 10% respectively. How you arrive at 25% and 0% is by deducting the tax credit when you do your tax calculation. This is best illustrated by means of some examples.

As we've said, when an individual receives a dividend, the amount received is 'grossed up' by the fraction 10/9 and this is known as the gross dividend. The gross dividend is taxed along with the taxpayer's other income.

Example 1 – Basic-rate taxpayer
John receives a £90 dividend. His tax calculation is as follows:

Gross Dividend: £90 x 10/9	*£100*
Tax @ 10%	*£10*
Tax credit: £100 x 10%	*£10*
Tax payable	*£0*

Example 2 – Higher-rate taxpayer
Jack a higher-rate taxpayer receives a dividend of £90. His tax calculation is as follows:

Gross Dividend: £90 x 10/9	*£100*
Tax @ 32.5%	*£32.50*
Tax credit: £100 x 10%	*£10*
Tax payable	*£22.5*

Jack has actually received £90. Out of this he will have to pay £22.50 to the Inland Revenue. The effective tax rate is therefore 22.5/90 = 25%.

If your dividend income pushes you into the higher-rate tax bracket, your effective tax rate on your dividend income will lie somewhere between 0% and 25%. To see why, it's first important to have a firm grasp of UK income tax rates.

UK Income Tax Rates

For the 2005/2006 tax year the following tax rates apply:

	£
• Starting rate - 10%	First 2,090
• Basic rate - 22%	Next 30,310
• Higher rate – 40%	Over 32,400

In addition, everyone enjoys a personal allowance of £4,895, which means the first £4,895 of income you receive is completely tax free. What this means is that you only pay tax at 40% when you earn more than £37,295 (£32,400 + £4,895).

It's also important to point out that dividends are the 'top slice' of income so if you earn salary or other income such as rents and interest of more than £37,295, all of your dividends will be taxed at the higher rate.

Now let's see how much tax an investor pays who earns all his income from dividends.

Example 1

Phil receives dividends of £45,000 and no other income. How is his tax calculated?

	£
Gross Dividends £45,000 x 100/90	*50,000*
Less: Personal allowance	*4,895*
Taxable income	*45,105*
Tax @ 10% on first £2,090	*209*
Tax @ 10% on next £30,310	*3,031*
Tax @ 32.5% on balance £12,705	*4,129*
Total Tax	*7,369*
Less Tax Credit (10% Gross dividend)	*5,000*
Tax payable	*2,369*

In total Phil earns £45,000 in dividends and pays tax of £2,369 which is an effective tax rate of just 5.3%.

This example illustrates that dividends are an extremely tax efficient form of income. What about a taxpayer who earns income from a variety of sources. How much tax would this person end up paying?

Example 2

Pat received the following income during the 2005/06 tax year:

- *Salary from employment with Dingbat plc - £20,000*
- *Net rental income from buy-to-let properties - £8,000*
- *Bank interest - £2,000 (gross)*
- *Net dividends from shares in Rich plc - £10,000*

Income tax of £3,000 has already been deducted from his salary. His tax bill is calculated as follows:

Salary	*£20,000*
Rental income	*£8,000*
Interest	*£2,000*
Gross Dividends	*£11,111.11*
Total taxable income	*£41,111*
Less: personal allowance	*£4,895*
	£36,216

Tax on Salary	
£2,090 @ 10%	*£209*
£20,000 - £4,895 - £2,090 = £13,015 @ 22%	*£2,863*
Rental income	
£8,000 @ 22%	*£1,760*
Interest	
£2,000 @ 20%	*£400*
Dividends	
Balance of basic rate tax band:	
£32,400 – £2,090 – £13,015 – £8,000 – £2,000:	
£7,295 @ 10%	*£729.5*
Remainder taxed in higher rate band:	
£11,111.11 - £7,295:	
£3,816.11 @32.5%	*£1,240*
Total tax	***£7,201***
Less:	
Tax deducted on interest	*£400*
PAYE	*£3,000*
Dividend Tax Credit	*£1,111*
Total income tax payable	***£2,690***

In this example, Pat has received dividends totalling £10,000 and paid £858 in tax, after subtracting the dividend tax credit. The effective tax rate is just 8.5%.

Remember that dividends are treated as the final source of income when looking at which income to tax first. Therefore if you have dividends and your total income is over the higher rate band (£32,400 for the 2005/06 tax year), some or all of the dividends will be taxed at the higher rate.

Payments on Account

Most taxpayers only have to pay income tax on their dividends when they submit their annual tax return by January 31 each year.

However, if you earn a lot of income from dividends you may have to make two 'payments on account'. These are based on your income tax liability from the previous tax year and have to be paid by 31 January *during* the tax year and by 31 July *following* the tax year.

Payments on account are not necessary if:

- Your tax liability for the previous year (net of tax deducted at source) is less than £500, or
- More than 80% of your previous year's tax liability was met by tax deducted at source.

If you have substantial dividend income, or are a share trader, these provisions may therefore apply to you.

Note that interest, which is usually subject to deduction of tax at source, would not be included in assessing whether payments on account are due.

Income-splitting Opportunities

Spreading ownership of assets between a husband and wife is one of the best ways of avoiding both income tax and capital gains tax. In this section we'll focus on the opportunities to save income tax.

The reason it's possible to split income is that spouses are treated as separate individuals for tax purposes BUT they are allowed to transfer assets between each other with no capital gains tax arising.

To benefit it's important that one of the spouses earns less income than the other. The best case scenario is where one spouse is a higher-rate taxpayer (paying 25% tax on dividend income and 40% on rental profits and interest) and the other spouse earns no income at all.

Remember that, before tax has to be paid at the full rate, each UK resident individual is entitled to:

- A personal allowance, currently £4,895.
- A starting rate of income tax, currently 10% but 0% for dividend income.
- A basic rate, currently 22% but 0% for dividend income.

The key is to make sure that your spouse's income tax personal allowance and lower tax rates are fully utilized. In terms of dividends, this can mean the difference between a 25% effective tax rate and a 0% rate, just by ensuring that shares are owned by the right person at the right time.

In these circumstances, gifting assets to the low-income spouse will reap enormous tax savings. In certain circumstances there will be absolutely no tax payable at all!

Take the example of a married man who is a higher-rate taxpayer and owns shares which generate dividends of £30,000. He would normally pay £7,500 in income tax. If, however, his wife has no earnings, transferring all of the shares to her would completely eliminate this tax bill.

And remember transferring assets to your spouse has absolutely no capital gains tax consequences.

However, the capital gains tax position would need to be considered when you come to *sell* the shares. If 100% ownership is transferred to your spouse (rather than, say, 50%) only one capital gains tax exemption will be available when the shares are sold.

In other words, the best split for income tax savings may not be the best split for capital gains tax savings.

However, the good news is that you can have your cake and eat it! There's nothing to stop the lower earning spouse from owning all the shares while they are used to produce dividend income and then transferring 50% (or some other suitable percentage) back to the other spouse prior to sale.

Let's have a look at an example to illustrate the potential benefits.

Example

David has a well paid job in the city and holds share investments that produce net dividend income of £35,000. David will pay income tax of £8,750 on the dividend income as he is a higher-rate taxpayer.

He decides to transfer the shares to his wife, Sue, who earns no other income.

She would be entitled to the personal allowance of £4,895 and given that the remaining income falls solely within the basic rate band, the tax credit would cover any income tax liability. She would therefore have no income tax to pay on the £35,000 dividend income. This would be a tax saving for the couple of £8,750, enough to buy a small car!

To do this, 'beneficial title' to the shares must be transferred to the other spouse which some investors may not feel comfortable about.

One option is to make use of the '50:50' rule. Where investment assets are held jointly between husband and wife the Inland Revenue automatically assumes that the ownership and hence income is split 50:50, irrespective of the actual split between the spouses. In other words, one spouse can own 99% of the shares and the other spouse can earn 1%, with income split equally for tax purposes.

(This makes the Inland Revenue's job easier as it would be difficult to identify the true beneficial interests in many cases!)

Therefore, even if one owns 1%, and the remaining spouse owns 99% of a shareholding, the income would still be split 50:50.

Where investment assets are held jointly by spouses the 50:50 rule will apply unless the couple make a joint declaration that they want the actual beneficial interests to apply (this can be made on a form 17 - available from the Inland Revenue website).

Clearly, for our share investor who wishes to split income to save tax, without giving away significant title, the answer would be to not make such a declaration.

If 50:50 is not an aggressive enough split, and you want your spouse to be taxed on all the income, it is necessary to transfer beneficial ownership in all the shares.

Although, splitting ownership can result in greater income tax savings, it's important to point out that, if the shares are sold, capital gains tax will follow the actual beneficial interest, and not the 50:50 rule. In other words all or most of the gains will be taxed in the one spouse's hands. This could be disastrous because the couple will lose one capital gains tax exemption. Furthermore the balance will potentially be taxed at 40% rather than the lower capital gains tax rate of 20%.

It's also worthwhile noting that the 2004 budget has withdrawn the 50:50 rule for shares in close companies. Basically this will apply to unquoted and family companies where the company is controlled by the directors or fewer than five shareholders. In this case, the actual beneficial interests will be used to determine the income for each spouse.

Example

Jack is a higher-rate taxpayer and buys shares worth £100,000. He gifts his wife Emily, who earns no income, a 1% interest in the shares. Dividend income of £15,000 is received during the year.

Assuming no declaration is made by Jack and Emily, the 50:50 rule will apply.

They would each be assessed on income of £7,500, with Jack paying income tax of £1,875 and Emily paying no income tax. Jack has therefore saved himself £1,875 and only transferred 1% of the title.

It would however, be more effective for Jack to transfer all of the shares to his wife. She would then receive the dividends and there would be no income tax payable on the dividends.

However, because only one person owns the shares only one CGT annual exemption will be available when they come to sell.

What Jack and Emily want to do is to minimize both income tax and capital gains tax. To minimize capital gains tax, prior to selling, Emily should transfer sufficient shares so that Jack can make full use of his annual exemption.

For example, let's say Emily holds on to the shares for 10 years, at which point she decides to take her profits. Let's say the shares have increased in value to £200,000. She is therefore looking at a potential gain of £100,000.

Assuming the shares are non-business assets (eg, shares in a quoted company of which she is not an employee), the taper relief percentage would be 40%. This means 60% or £60,000 is taxable.

Assuming the annual exemption has risen to £10,000, Emily could transfer shares with a gain equivalent to £16,667 to Jack. This would be equivalent to a transfer of shares with a value of £33,334 (16.7% of her shareholding).

The remaining 83.3% would be taxed as follows:

	Jack	**Emily**
Proceeds	£33,334	£166,666
Less:		
Cost	£16,667	£83,333
Taper relief	£6,667	£33,333
Annual exemption	£10,000	£10,000
Taxable Gain	NIL	£40,000

This option would ensure that:

- The ongoing dividend income is taxed at the lowest rate.
- Both annual exemptions are available when the shares are sold.
- Emily gets to use any remaining basic-rate tax band when the shares are sold, therefore ensuring that part of the gain is taxed at 20% as opposed to 40% if all the shares were owned by Jack.

Although this is perfectly legitimate tax planning, it would be wise not to transfer the interest immediately prior to selling the shares. Although unlikely, the Inland Revenue could challenge the transfer in such a circumstance on anti-avoidance grounds. This type of tax planning will therefore work best where the transfer was a suitable period prior to a disposal, and no actions had yet been taken to dispose of the shares.

Using Your Children to Reduce Tax

Once your spouse's personal allowance and lower and basic-rate tax bands are used up, what next? Can you transfer income to your children? Unfortunately there are two key differences between the tax treatment of spouses and children.

First, a transfer of shares to children would be classed as a disposal for capital gains tax purposes, and the disposal proceeds would be deemed to be the market value of the shares. This could result in a hefty capital gains tax bill.

Second, when the income exceeds £100 there is tax anti-avoidance legislation that treats income from assets gifted to children as the parent's income.

So, for example, if there is a transfer of shares from a father to his son, the income will be taxed in the son's hands only if it is less than £100 per year. If it's more than that, the whole of the dividend payment will be taxed in the father's hands. Given that he will already have paid capital gains tax on the transfer of the shares, this would be a disastrous state of affairs.

So are there any ways to circumvent these rules?

Well, firstly, it only applies to *income tax* and only where the income is more than £100. So a father could transfer shares which are expected to generate significant capital gains rather than dividend income.

When the children sell the shares the profits will be subject to capital gains tax. However, the potential tax bill could be quite low because children of any age qualify for an annual capital gains tax allowance. Furthermore, if your children have no other income, any gains that are taxable could be subject to 10% or 20% rather than 40%.

Note that it does not make sense to purchase shares and then transfer them to children, especially if they're showing good profits already. First, your profits will be subject to capital gains tax. Second, after a few years taper relief is only just starting to kick in. If you sell your shares the 'taper relief clock' is reset and you have to start all over again. The best bet would be to consider one of the following strategies:

- Transfer cash to your children so they can buy the shares directly.
- Immediately transfer shares after you have bought them and before any gain arises.
- Purchase the shares purely as a nominee. There would need to be a written agreement substantiating this. Tax would then be payable by the beneficial owner of the shares. As the parent would be the owner of only the legal title to the shares (ie in 'name only'), the gain would be taxed in the hands of the child.

Secondly, when it comes to circumventing these rules, it is important to remember that they only apply to children *under 18 years of age*.

If your children are over 18 you can transfer shares to them and the income will be taxed in their hands. Of course, this isn't much use if your children are themselves higher-rate taxpayers. However, a great many parents will be in the situation where their adult children are either studying or, if in work, paying tax at the basic rate. In these circumstances there is scope to save income tax by transferring shares to them.

If your adult children are higher-rate taxpayers but have spouses who earn little or no income, tax savings could be achieved by transferring shares directly to their spouses. Of course this is not always desirable for reasons that have nothing to do with tax. However, many young couples who earn significantly different amounts of income have very few income-producing assets which let them split income and make full use of the 'poorer' spouse's personal allowance and basic rate tax band. This is one way they can.

Remember that you will have to pay capital gains tax on any profits when you make the transfer and so may want to consider following one of the three strategies outlined above.

Third, the anti-avoidance rules only apply to parents transferring income-producing assets to their children. They do not apply to *grandparents* (or uncles and aunts etc) who gift shares to grandchildren.

Note that any gift would need to be a *bona fide* gift. If the gift was in fact a sham and, for example, the share proceeds were passed pack to the adult who gifted them in the first place, the Inland Revenue would argue that the beneficial interest always remained with them and tax them accordingly.

Therefore, transfers of shares would be useful for grandparents, in particular, who wish to transfer assets to their grandchildren and reduce their estates for inheritance tax purposes.

Example

Pete and Ethel have three grandchildren. They have a substantial estate, and amongst their various investments have £500,000 invested in an unquoted trading company.

This produces net dividend income of £50,000 per year. As they are both higher-rate taxpayers, the income tax charge would be £12,500.

They decide to transfer the shares to their three grandchildren. They will each receive shares worth £167,667, with annual dividend income of £16,667. As they have no other income they would pay no tax on the dividends.

Note that in this example, unquoted trading shares were used, which we have assumed would enable the shares to qualify for gift relief on the transfer to the grandchildren (see Chapter 22 on inheritance tax planning). If gift relief was not available, this may make the transfer of the shares a no go, given the potential capital gains tax liability that will arise when the shares are transferred.

However all is not lost. If the shares are in a regular quoted company Pete and Ethel could treat the transfer to the grandchildren as more of a long-term exercise and realize just enough profit to make use of their annual capital gains tax allowances (about £17,000 per year).

Using a Company to Avoid Income Tax

Using a company to invest in shares is considered in detail in Chapter 24, but primarily with respect to capital gains tax planning. However, in certain circumstances using a company could also be beneficial from an income tax perspective.

The reason using a company may be useful from an income tax position is that dividends received by a company from another UK company are completely tax free.

The extraction of cash from the share investment company would itself be taxable, and if the cash was extracted as a dividend, there would be no difference between receiving the dividend directly or from your own company.

One long-term strategy could be to use a company as a 'money box' entity. Dividends could be saved up over many years until a sizeable cash balance develops. For example, let's say you earn £15,000 of dividends per year. After 10 years you will have accumulated £150,000 worth of dividends with a tax saving of about £37,500.

Extraction of the funds in the UK would result in an income tax charge. However the sole shareholder could become non-UK resident and declare a large dividend. As a non-resident individual this would be likely to be 'exempt' from UK income tax with the notional tax credit completely satisfying any income tax liability.

Problems with Money Box Companies

The problem here would be finding a country that you would want to live in for a period and that would not tax the dividends more than in the UK.

Note that whilst anti-avoidance provisions require an individual to generally be non-resident for five complete years to avoid UK capital gains tax, no such provision exists for income tax, and it would therefore be theoretically possible to become non-resident for a tax year during which the dividend was declared before moving back to the UK.

In practice, capital gains tax considerations would be likely to dominate this type of tax planning. For example, by using a UK company the company would remain within the charge to UK corporation tax, whereas by owning the shares personally, UK CGT could be avoided by becoming non-resident for five complete tax years.

There would also be the status of the company to consider. The company would need to either be a trading or investment company (or a combination) to gain a deduction for any costs. A passive holding of shares would certainly not qualify as a trading company and would probably not qualify as an investment company either.

Whereas this would not be relevant as regards dividend income of the company (as this would not be taxable), any future gains realized by the company would be taxed in full with no deduction for the expenses of running the company that would ordinarily be available to a trading or investment company.

In addition, the Close Investment Company provisions would apply so that any gain would be taxed in the company at a standard 30% (as these provisions do not apply just to investment companies).

Therefore, although a company could be used to mitigate tax on ongoing income, specialist advice would undoubtedly need to be taken and the CGT implications would need close inspection.

Chapter 22

How to Avoid Inheritance Tax

It's bad enough having to pay tax on your income or gains once, but twice? That surely isn't fair! Unfortunately this is exactly what happens with inheritance tax.

In simple terms, your net assets (that's everything you own less your debts and other liabilities) are subject to inheritance tax at a rate of 40% to the extent that they exceed the 'nil rate band'. The nil rate band for the 2005/2006 tax year is £275,000.

Because your assets will have generally been purchased out of after-tax income, the assets are in effect being taxed twice.

It is this aspect of inheritance tax that offends so many people. You've worked hard and paid your taxes throughout your lifetime, yet the government still wants to take a large chunk of your estate when you die.

In this chapter we'll look at how IHT operates and the main reliefs and opportunities available to enable you to minimise any charge, with particular reference to share investors.

Who is Affected by Inheritance Tax?

Everybody who is either UK domiciled or has UK assets, provided the estate is above the £275,000 nil rate band is potentially affected.

'Estate' is a wide term and includes any asset that the deceased was beneficially entitled to. This will therefore commonly include:

- Land and property
- Bank and building society deposits

- Shares and securities
- Debtors
- Personal chattels

Note that it is *domicile* that is important here. Your *residence* is irrelevant and you could easily be non-resident yet UK domiciled (For more information about domicile see Chapter 19). In fact, because losing your UK domicile is much more difficult than losing your UK residence, there are many people who would be subject to UK inheritance tax but not subject to UK capital gains tax!

For inheritance tax purposes you are also deemed to be UK domiciled if either:

- You are UK resident for 17 out of the last 20 years, or
- You have lost your UK domicile within the last three years.

These deemed domicile rules, especially the first one, are especially important for non-UK domiciliaries who become UK resident for a significant period (for example, if you moved here from Australia many years ago). If you're not careful, the estate will fall into the UK inheritance tax net.

A UK domiciled individual is subject to inheritance tax on the value of his or her entire worldwide estate. Therefore, where your assets are located is irrelevant for inheritance purposes. If you are UK domiciled, your entire estate will be subject to inheritance tax.

Therefore the benefit of using any offshore structures will be reduced as your estate will include offshore accounts and shares in overseas companies.

However, a non-UK domiciliary is only subject to UK IHT on the value of his or her UK estate. This means that only UK assets will be classed within the definition of 'estate'.

Location of Assets

The courts have established through a number of decisions where various assets are deemed to be located. The key points are:

- Shares and securities are situated where they are registered. If they are transferable upon more than one register, they are situated where they would normally be dealt with in the ordinary course of business. If the shares are in unquoted companies, they would be located where the company in question is located.
- Government securities are situated at the place of registration.
- Bearer shares and securities used to be located where the document of title was kept. Changes in the 2005 Budget now locate the shares where the company is registered.
- Bank accounts are situated at the branch which maintains the account. However, a foreign currency account with a recognised bank in the UK is exempt from UK IHT on the death of an individual who is non-UK resident/ordinarily resident and non-UK domiciled.

There is therefore an opportunity for a non-domiciliary to avoid UK inheritance tax by using offshore accounts and holding shares in offshore companies. This is a perfectly acceptable method of arranging your tax affairs and could lead to a drastically reduced IHT charge.

Non-UK domiciliaries can also use an offshore company or trust to invest in UK shares. The taxpayer would then own shares in an overseas asset (the offshore company) as opposed to the underlying UK shares and, as such, the value of the UK shares held would be excluded from the estate. See Chapter 19 for further details on the overseas tax planning.

Each person is entitled to use the nil rate band which exempts a proportion of the estate from IHT. For the 2005/2006 tax year this amount is £275,000. The remaining estate is then taxed at 40%.

However, it is not just the assets held at the date of death that need to be taken into consideration. If you have made any gifts in the seven years prior to your death, these are deducted from the nil rate band, which will result in more of your estate falling into the tax net.

Example

Jack, a UK domiciled individual, died on September 15 2005. He had shareholdings in numerous UK quoted companies, which had a market value of £100,000 at the date of his death. He also had other assets amounting to £100,000. He had no liabilities.

On 30 September 2003, he had given his grandson shares worth £100,000. The shares have done well and now have a market value of £200,000.

Jack's inheritance tax bill (ignoring any reliefs/exemptions) is calculated as follows:

Assets	*£200,000*
Nil rate band	*£275,000*
Less: utilised in 2003 gift	*£100,000*
Remaining	*£175,000*
Taxable estate	*£25,000*
Inheritance tax @ 40%	*£10,000*

Taper Relief

If you survive seven years after making a gift it will not be included in your estate for inheritance tax purposes. However, partial relief is available if you survive for at least three years.

The various rates of taper relief are as follows:

3-4 years	20%
4-5 years	40%
5-6 years	60%
6-7 years	80%

Therefore if you survive for six years and eight months after making a large gift, 80% of the value of the gift will be exempt from inheritance tax.

It's also important to point out that the first £3,000 of any asset transfers in each tax year is exempt from inheritance tax.

Example

Wilf, aged 92, gave shares in King plc to his son in May 2003 when they had a market value of £100,000. He had made gifts in the previous seven years that exceeded the nil rate band. He dies on November 8 2008.

The value of the gift for IHT purposes will be:

	£
Value at date of gift	*100,000*
Less: annual exemptions:	
2003/2004	*3,000*
2004/2005	*3,000*
Value of gift	*94,000*

The tax on the gift would normally be calculated at 40% ie £37,600. However, as the gift was made five to six years before Wilf's death, it will qualify for taper relief of £22,560 (60% x £37,600).
The total inheritance tax payable will be £15,040 (£37,600 - £22,560).

Appreciating Assets

Note that the value of shares taken into account for inheritance tax purposes is their value at the date the gift is made and NOT at the date of death.

This value is 'locked in' even if the shares double or treble. Therefore if you gifted them when they were worth 5p each, the fact that they are valued at 15p at the date of your death will not be relevant. Similarly, if you gift them when they are worth £1 each the fact that they are valued at 1p at the date of your death will also not be relevant.

Hence from an inheritance tax planning perspective it is generally better to gift shares that you regard as undervalued, for example after a severe market downturn.

This 'gift now' strategy also enables maximum use of the seven-year exemption or the taper relief rates.

Example

Debbie has shares valued at £500,000. She is considering transferring them to her daughter in March 2006. Assuming annual capital growth of 10%, and assuming she owns other assets that would use up her nil rate band, the inheritance tax charge if she holds on to her shares instead of gifting them would be as follows:

Year of Death	***Value of shares***	***Inheritance Tax***
	£	***£***
March 2007	*550,000*	*220,000*
March 2008	*605,000*	*242,000*
March 2009	*665,500*	*266,200*
March 2010	*732,050*	*292,820*
March 2011	*805,255*	*322,102*
March 2012	*885,781*	*354,312*
March 2013	*974,359*	*389,744*
March 2014	*1,071,794*	*428,718*

However, if Debbie gifted the shares to her daughter in March 2006, the tax charge would be as follows:

Year of Death	***Value of shares***	***Inheritance Tax***
	£	***£***
March 2007	*500,000*	*220,000*
March 2008	*500,000*	*220,000*
March 2009	*500,000*	*176,000*
March 2010	*500,000*	*132,000*
March 2011	*500,000*	*88,000*
March 2012	*500,000*	*44,000*
March 2013	*500,000*	*0*
March 2014	*500,000*	*0*

By simply acting sooner rather than later, some significant tax savings can be made and in this case Debbie can save inheritance tax of around £428,000 by immediately transferring the shares.

However, matters are not always that simple. There are a number of issues to be considered before accepting this strategy:

- The shares will then belong to the person to whom the shares have been gifted, and they will receive dividends and be entitled to dispose of the shares as they wish. The income tax considerations will therefore also need to be considered.
- Capital gains tax may have to be paid. The transfer of the shares to anyone except a spouse would be a chargeable event for CGT purposes. That's why it's better to transfer shares appreciating in value earlier, as any gain is likely to be small.

  If the shares are transferred to a beneficiary on death, CGT is irrelevant, as death is not a chargeable event for CGT purposes. Therefore any gain would be wiped out and the beneficiary would inherit the shares with a cost for CGT purposes equivalent to the probate value (in other words, market value at death). Of course, the downside is that the value of the shares then is subject to a flat rate inheritance tax charge at 40% to the extent that their value exceeds the nil rate band.

When looking at reducing your overall tax position there is a trade off between capital gains tax and inheritance tax. Thanks to the various reliefs and deductions available in many cases a gift of shares which results in capital gains tax being paid will be more tax efficient than retaining the shares and incurring an IHT charge – although, as ever, this depends on the particular circumstances.

Example

Fred owns shares with a value of £200,000. He has other assets that would use up his the nil rate band, so we can assume that he faces a potential IHT charge of £80,000 on the shares if he holds on to them and passes them to his son on his death.

He acquired them for £50,000 three years previously, so the gain we're looking at is £150,000 before reliefs. The tables below compare the capital gains tax and inheritance tax faced by Fred/his estate, dependent on whether he gifts the shares or holds on to them.

Retaining the Shares

Assuming a growth in value of 10% per annum.

Year of death	***Value of shares***	***IHT charge***
1	*£220,000*	*£88,000*
2	*£242,000*	*£96,800*
3	*£266,200*	*£106,480*
4	*£292,820*	*£117,128*
5	*£322,102*	*£128,841*
6	*£354,312*	*£141,725*
7	*£389,743*	*£155,897*
8	*£428,717*	*£171,487*

Gifting the Shares

If Fred gifted the shares to his son in year one, he would suffer a CGT charge of £57,000 (taking into account 5% taper relief as he had owned the shares for three years already).

Year of death	*Value of shares*	*IHT charge*
1	*£200,000*	*£80,000*
2	*£200,000*	*£80,000*
3	*£200,000*	*£80,000*
4	*£200,000*	*£64,000*
5	*£200,000*	*£48,000*
6	*£200,000*	*£32,000*
7	*£200,000*	*£16,000*
8	*£200,000*	*£0*

In this case, by immediately gifting the shares, Fred suffers a CGT charge of £57,000. But if he survives for eight years, there would then be no IHT charge. This is significantly less than holding on to the shares and passing them as a bequest (a saving of over £114,000 in total tax!). Similarly, if Fred had survived for five years after the date of the gift, the total tax charge would have been £105,000, still substantially less than the £128,841 tax charge if he held on to the shares.

In this example, if the person died within four years of the date of the gift, there would have been no benefit in making the gift. However, this example is for illustrative purposes and is based on a large gain with only low rates of taper relief. If the gain was smaller, if business asset taper relief applied or if the ownership period prior to the gift was longer, this would also tilt the balance in favour of a gift in the early years.

Gift with Reservation of Benefit (GROB)

We've looked at the benefits of gifting shares to reduce inheritance tax. The problem is that you may not actually want to lose the dividend income just yet. It could be tempting to gift the legal title, yet ensure that you still obtain the dividend income.

Any attempt to retain benefits associated with share ownership (such as having the dividend income transferred into your bank account) would open up the possibility of the Inland Revenue treating the gift as a GROB and including the shares in your estate when calculating your inheritance tax bill.

The gift would therefore be totally ineffective as a means of reducing inheritance tax.

Any transfer of shares should be a *bona fide* transfer and not a 'sham' arrangement designed to avoid tax. You would need to ensure that the beneficial interest in the shares was also transferred. This beneficial interest would include the right to receive dividend income, and the right to dispose of the shares.

IHT Reliefs and Deductions

Just as with capital gains tax, there are a number of reliefs available that can help you reduce your likely inheritance tax bill.

Remember that your estate includes your liabilities so if you have a heavily leveraged/geared portfolio, the actual value of the shares included in your estate could be far lower.

In fact, borrowing money can be a useful tax-planning technique, as it can reduce the estate's value for inheritance tax purposes, yet avoid the crystallisation of a capital gains tax charge when shares are gifted.

Example

Let's assume Joan has shares valued at £250,000. The value of her remaining estate exceeds the nil rate band. The shares were originally purchased for £25,000.

Her estate is therefore faced with a potential inheritance tax charge of £100,000 if she holds on to the shares, or a £90,000 capital gains tax charge if she gifts them to a relative.

One tax-efficient option would be to raise finance of £200,000 and gift this amount to her son or other relative. This would be a potentially exempt transfer and, as such, exempt from IHT after seven years (with taper relief building up after three years). The net value of her estate would be reduced by £200,000 and capital gains tax would not be payable because the gift was cash.

Annual IHT Exemption

Any transfers made during the tax year that are less than £3,000 are free of inheritance tax. If the value gifted exceeds this, any unused annual exemption from the previous year can be brought forward (for one year only).

This can therefore be a useful method of withdrawing small sums from an individual's estate over a number of years. As shareholdings are by their nature divisible, gifts of shares are particularly suited to making use of the annual exemption.

Indeed anybody looking to reduce the value of their estate should be taking advantage of this tax break.

Example

Rob gave shares in Hol plc, with a market value of £10,000, to his niece on 17 May 2005. He had made no previous gifts.

He will be entitled to deduct the annual exemption for the 2005/2006 tax year and also the annual exemption for the 2004/2005 tax year, as this was unused and can be carried forward for one year. The element of gift taken into account for IHT purposes would be £4,000.

Remember that this gift would only be subject to IHT if his estate was above the nil rate band and if he were to die before 17 May 2012.

Gifts in Consideration of Marriage

When a marriage takes place parents can gift the child £5,000, grandparents can gift £2,500 and remoter relatives can gift £1,000, and these amounts will fall out of the inheritance tax net. These amounts are over and above the annual exemption.

Example

Harry, decides to transfer his shares worth £10,000 to his daughter as a wedding present. Assuming that Harry has made no previous transfers, he will be entitled to deduct the £5,000 marriage exemption and the current and previous years' annual exemptions, which will more than cover the value of the shares gifted. This gift will therefore be ignored for inheritance tax purposes.

Note that there are also additional minor reliefs such as the small gifts exemption which excludes from IHT small gifts of up to £250 per year.

Business Property Relief (BPR)

Certain shares can be passed on totally free from inheritance tax because they qualify for Business Property Relief (BPR).

The relief is available provided the following conditions are met:

- The asset is 'relevant business property', and
- The asset must be owned by the person making the transfer for the last two years at least.

What is Relevant Business Property?

There are various types of property that qualify for BPR. However, as regards shares, 'relevant business property' includes:

- Shares in unquoted companies, provided the company does not deal in shares or land). These qualify for 100% relief.

- Shares in quoted companies (again the company must not deal in shares or land), provided the transferor controls the company. These qualify for 50% relief.

Note that the company must also be a trading company - shares in investment companies do not qualify for business property relief. For more information about trading and investment companies see Chapter 24.

AIM listed shares are treated as unquoted for this purpose. Therefore provided the company is a trading company and you've owned the shares for at least two years, you should be entitled to full BPR.

As regards quoted company shares, the requirement that you must control the company to qualify for BPR excludes the vast majority of investors from this relief.

If you have assets that do qualify for BPR, this will immediately change your inheritance tax planning actions, as the shares would be effectively exempt from IHT whether gifted or retained until death.

In this case, there is no tax advantage in gifting the shares 'sooner rather than later' as they would be exempt in any case. In fact, it would be better to hold on to the shares, as this would allow the shares to be passed on to relatives free from capital gains tax.

Chapter 23

The Tax Benefits of Being a 'Share Trader'

There is a big difference between what stock market enthusiasts mean by the terms 'share trader' and 'share investor' and what the taxman takes these words to mean.

The distinction in UK tax law between trading and investing doesn't just apply to buying and selling financial assets - it's a general concept that relates to all activities.

A share trader is taxed in a completely different manner to a share investor. The fundamental difference is that a trader will hold shares as his 'stock', much as a motor dealer holds cars or a supermarket holds cans of beans. In comparison, an investor is believed to hold shares as assets, which are used to generate income – dividend income in this case.

The most important difference between share traders and share investors is that share traders pay *income tax* whereas share investors pay *capital gains tax.*

More specifically, share traders are taxed under 'Schedule D Case I' of the income tax legislation, which sets out the rules for calculating taxable profits for all trading operations.

As a self-employed individual, the trader also has obligations to pay national insurance and is entitled to establish a personal pension scheme.

So which is better, being classed as a trader or an investor?

That's the million-dollar question and, as always with tax, there is no easy answer. It will depend on your personal circumstances – you have to weigh up the pros and cons and decide which tax is better for YOU.

To help you answer this important question, however, we'll take a detailed look at the pros and cons of being classified as a trader, followed by some detailed numerical comparisons of trading versus investment.

First, however, it's essential to explain what factors the Inland Revenue takes into consideration when deciding whether you are a 'trader' or an 'investor'.

Trading vs Investment

From the taxman's standpoint, an investor acquires an asset with the intention of generating *income*. For example, a share investor would buy shares to generate dividend income. Making a profit from selling the asset is supposed to be a secondary consideration. A trader, on the other hand, buys shares with the intention of selling them at a profit.

However, intention is a difficult concept for the tax authorities to get a grip on. And your own opinion of your intention will certainly not be a decisive factor! Instead the taxman uses a variety of practical pointers to decide whether you are a trader or investor. These are commonly known as the 'badges of trade'.

If you ask the Inland Revenue whether you are a share trader or a share investor, they will probably refer you to these badges of trade.

The Inland Revenue will look firstly at your motive in buying and selling and then at the transaction in question to try and obtain a full picture of your activities.

Motive of the Taxpayer

Your motive in buying and selling shares is crucial, although it is difficult to actually prove to the Inland Revenue's satisfaction. Typical practical matters that the Inland Revenue will look at include:

- Whether the share purchase is an isolated event.
- Whether or not buying and selling shares is your only 'occupation'.
- Whether you reinvest your profits to buy more shares.
- The amount of capital that you have invested in your sharedealing activities. For example it would perhaps be easier to persuade the Inland Revenue that you were a trader if you had trading capital in excess of £50,000 - £75,000.

The Actual Transaction

Inland Revenue will also look at the circumstances of the actual transaction to identify whether any aspect of this indicates a trading motive.

In particular they will assess:

- The length of time between the purchase of the shares and the disposal of the shares.
- The frequency of the share transactions. This will be a KEY factor in practice. Inland Revenue will be looking for evidence of a 'continuous and habitual' activity.
- Whether the shares were purchased or simply acquired by way of an inheritance or through some other channel.
- The reason for the sale. The sale of the shares to cover a financial 'emergency' may make the likelihood of the transaction being classed as trading less likely.
- Are you claiming a tax loss? Trying to persuade the Inland Revenue that you are a trader when you have incurred a sizeable loss on share dealing activities would be much more difficult than if there were taxable profits.

- Whether any finance was obtained for the share purchases or to fund the share trading activity, for example office costs and computer equipment. A large loan to purchase shares may mean that the interest payments would offset the dividend payments. In such a case there would be good grounds for arguing that the sole opportunity to make a profit would be to dispose of the shares. This would then increase the likelihood of a trading motive.
- Dividend policy of the company in question. If the company has historically paid no dividends, this would strengthen your argument for trading status, as you would be looking to dispose of the shares to realise a profit.
- Type of shares/securities purchased. Shares that pay no income might be more easily viewed as trading than investment assets.
- Do your share dealing activities resemble a trading operation?

That last point point is crucial and in a sense sums up all the other factors. Does the taxpayer give the appearance of carrying on a trade? Or as one judge put it, what we're looking for is a *"deliberate and organised scheme of profit making"*.

The buying and selling frequency, amount of capital invested, method of financing and so on all point to whether you are engaged in a 'scheme of profit making', and it is these factors in which the Inland Revenue is most interested.

Unfortunately it's not possible to simply write a list of actions you should take which will guarantee trading status. If you want to classify yourself as a share trader, you would need to complete your tax return on that basis with your share profits being regarded as trading income. I would suggest that you make clear what you are doing in a letter accompanying your tax return, allowing the Inland Revenue the opportunity to review your position if required.

You would have to build a 'pack' of evidence to support your trading status, considering as many of the above factors as possible.

Financial Assets vs Other Assets

To successfully convince the Inland Revenue that your activities constitute trading you have to overcome the general presumption held by the Inland Revenue that the purchase of income-producing assets would *usually* be classed as investing.

From the taxman's standpoint, shares are more likely to be held as investments. In particular, one judge has said:

"... Where the question is whether an individual engaged in speculative dealings in securities is carrying on a trade, the prima facie presumption would be ... that he is not."

Clearly if there are other 'badges of trade' that apply, the presumption against trading could be reversed. Although there is a presumption against trading, this is not the end of the matter. By following the right approach you can obtain trading status.

If you have a job in the financial markets this does not automatically mean your private share dealings will be classed as trading. Again, it will depend on the application of the general principles to assess whether you are actually in business on your own account and purchasing shares with the intention of resale at a profit.

Having said this, being employed in an associated industry would certainly be another 'card in your hand' and when combined with other relevant factors would strengthen a trading argument.

Summary

There is no single test you have to pass to be treated as a share trader. Instead your overall circumstances will be examined.

The main 'badges of trade' that will be looked at are:

- Frequency of buying and selling.
- The amount of capital at stake.
- How you came to own the shares. (Did you buy them yourself or were they received as a gift?)
- Type of shares purchased, for example, ones that generate no income.
- Method of finance.
- Whether you are claiming trading loss relief.
- Whether your activities resemble a trading operation.

So why would you want to be classed as a trader rather than an investor, or vice-versa? In the sections that follow we list most of the benefits and drawbacks of share trader status, followed by some detailed numerical comparisons.

Share Trading - Advantages

Expenses

One of the main advantages of being taxed as a share trader is that a claim can be made to offset any expenses incurred 'wholly and exclusively' for the purposes of the share trading activity.

This is a potentially wide provision and could allow a whole variety of additional expenses to be claimed - provided they each satisfy the 'wholly and exclusively' requirement.

Remember that for a share *investor*, the costs that can be deducted when calculating capital gains tax are restricted to the actual purchase cost of the shares and the other incidental expenses of buying and selling (usually just stamp duty and broker's fees).

This therefore gives a share trader a tremendous advantage over a share investor.

Types of expenses that could be claimed include:

- Office rent
- Utility bills and council tax
- Interest on a loan for the purposes of the trade. This could include a loan used to buy shares or the funds could be used to purchase equipment that would be used in the trade (for example, office equipment and computers).
- Capital allowances (discussed below).
- Professional subscriptions.
- Research materials, including books and share magazines.
- Share dealing expenses such as stockbroker fees.
- Stamp duty.
- Employee salaries.
- Online share services, eg access to premium share bulletin boards.

For a serious share dealer the opportunity to offset these additional expenses against the trading income could tip the scales and make share trader tax treatment most beneficial.

This is particularly the case where you deal in shares as a serious and organised activity on a frequent basis, in other words if you are a full-time professional trader. It's this type of person who will enjoy the most tax savings from share trader treatment.

Example

Steven disposes of shares worth £300,000 during the 2005/2006 tax year. The cost of these shares including dealing fees and stamp duty was £175,000. Steven is therefore looking at a profit of £125,000.

Let's assume he is classified as an investor and holds the shares jointly with his wife to take advantage of the two annual capital gains tax exemptions (currently £8,500 per person) and that they are both higher-rate taxpayers. The remaining gain of £108,000 would be taxed at 40% and capital gains tax of £43,200 would be payable.

Now let's assume Steven has no other employment and share trading is his full time activity. We'll also assume he incurs the following expenses:

- *Subscription to share trading website* — *£2,080*
- *Office rent* — *£25,000*
- *Investment analysis* — *£17,000*
- *Council tax* — *£2,500*
- *Utility bills* — *£1,500*
- *Share trading books* — *£750*
- *Share charting software* — *£2,000*

After deducting these expenses he would have a trading profit of £74,170. Again assuming Steven is a 40% taxpayer, his tax bill would be £29,668.

Therefore by being classified as a trader rather than an investor Steven has saved over £13,500 in tax.

Although Steven has made big tax savings you'll notice that he has very high costs. If his costs were far lower the tax savings would also be far lower and share trader tax treatment would be less appealing. We return to this later.

Capital Allowances

When you buy an asset that is used in your trade, the business is given capital allowances, which allow a percentage of the cost to be 'released' each year and treated as a tax-deductible expense.

There are many different capital allowances, depending on the nature of the asset. The most important one for share traders would be the plant and machinery allowance.

Plant and Machinery Allowances (P&M)

Plant means assets that:

- Perform a function within the business
- Have a degree of permanence
- Are used to carry on the business.

The assets most likely to qualify for plant and machinery allowances in this case would be computers and office equipment. The rate of tax relief is 25% per year, calculated on the 'reducing balance' basis.

Example

An item of plant purchased for £10,000 would qualify for capital allowances as follows:

Year 1 (25% x £10,000)	*£2,500*
Year 2 (25% x (£10,000 - £2,500)	*£1,875*
Year 3 (25% x (£10,000 - £4,375)	*£1,406*

...and so on.

There is also a first-year allowance available (FYA) that gives you a 50% deduction for the first year only, provided the equipment is bought between 1 April 2004 and 31 March 2005. Thereafter the 25% reducing balance basis applies. Therefore a share dealer who spends money on a new computer system would be entitled to a 50% deduction of the cost in the period the computer was purchased. A share investor purchasing the identical computer system would not be eligible for any tax relief.

Pension Contributions

Profits from a share dealing trade are classed as 'net relevant income' for the purposes of making pension fund contributions, which qualify for attractive tax relief.

The maximum amount that you can invest in the current tax year depends on your age and your net relevant earnings. The following table shows the percentage of net relevant earnings that can be invested:

Age on April 6	% of Earnings
Under 35	17.5
36-45	20
46-50	25
51-55	30
56-60	35
61+	40

Note that there is a minimum level of £3,600 that most UK resident individuals can invest. This is irrespective of the actual level of income during the year. This means that many share investors also qualify for a certain amount of tax relief on pension contributions.

All allowable contributions attract 22% tax relief at source. So, for a gross contribution of £10,000, a sum of £7,800 is paid to the pension provider. The pension provider credits the extra £2,200 to the plan and subsequently claims this back from the taxman.

Higher rate taxpayers claim on their tax returns for additional relief of 18%.

From April 6 2006 pensions will become a lot more attractive with bigger contribution limits and more investment flexibility. Details of these reforms are contained in the Taxcafe guide *Retire Rich with a Property Pension.*

Trading Losses

Capital losses are examined in Chapter 12. Broadly speaking, they are either offset against current year gains or carried forward to offset against future capital gains. Losses incurred in a trade are much more flexible. They can be:

- Offset against other income earned during the tax year.
- Carried forward against future profits arising from the same trade.
- Carried back against income earned in the previous tax year.
- Offset against capital gains in certain circumstances.

In summary, trading losses can be offset against other sources of income such as your salary (capital losses can not) and can lead to a tax refund (excess capital losses can only be carried forward for use in future tax years).

Example 1

Patrick deals in shares. He is a 40% taxpayer. His tax position for tax years 2002/2003 - 2005/2006 is as follows:

	Taxable profit	***Tax paid***
2002/2003	*£30,000*	*£12,000*
2003/2004	*£45,000*	*£18,000*
2004/2005	*-£20,000*	*NIL*
2005/2006	*£5,000*	*£2,000*

The loss incurred in 2004/2005 could be carried back to 2003/2004. This would therefore give rise to a repayment of income tax of £8,000. By contrast if Patrick was classed as a share investor, the loss would be carried forward to 2005/2006 and then only £5,000 would be offset.

Example 2

Jack is employed as a City broker. In the 2005/2006 tax year he earns a salary of £60,000. Tax deducted is approximately £16,000. Jack is a keen share trader and spends all his spare time playing the stock market. Unfortunately for Jack, his shares have taken a hammering, and he realises a loss of £30,000. This loss will be offset against his employment income for the period and his revised tax charge will be:

Income	*£60,000*
Loss	*£30,000*
Personal allowance	*£4,895*
Income	*£25,105*
£2,090@10%	*£209*
£23,015@22%	*£5,063*

He has already paid £16,000 in tax so he is entitled to a refund of £10,727.

Personal Allowance

If you have earned no other income during the tax year, you will be entitled to offset your personal allowance (£4,895 for the 2005/2006 tax year) against your trading profits.

If all your income comes from capital gains you are entitled to use up your 10% starting-rate tax band and your 22% basic-rate tax band but you are not entitled to a personal allowance.

Share Identification Rules

The share matching rules (see Chapter 4) only apply for capital gains tax purposes. This could give a share trader an added advantage over a share investor.

Remember that the matching rules for individuals match share sales with shares bought on:

- The same day
- The next 30 days
- After 5 April 1998
- The 1985 pool
- The 1982 pool

These rules do not apply to traders. Instead the normal rules regarding calculation of profits and losses would come into force.

Under normal accountancy principles, a share trader would therefore match shares on the basis of 'Last In First Out' (LIFO).

Example

Pat buys shares as follows:

- *31/05/2000* *5,000 at £1.90 each*
- *17/06/2003* *3,000 at £1.75 each*
- *19/08/2004* *5,000 at £2.10 each*
- *25/06/2005* *5,000 at £1.95 each*

He sells 5,000 shares on June 20 2005 for £2.20 each.

If the capital gains tax rules applied, Pat's disposal would be matched with the acquisition on 25 June 2005. The cost of the shares for tax purposes would be £1.95 each, resulting in a taxable profit of 25p per share. The taxable gain would therefore be £1,250 (5,000 x 25p).

However, if he is classed as a share trader, the disposal would be matched with the 2004 acquisition and the gain arising would be just £500.

Share Trading - Disadvantages

"Great," you might be thinking, "How do I persuade Inland Revenue that I'm a share trader?" Although the advantages above do seem quite impressive, this is not the whole story. As with most important tax decisions, there are benefits and drawbacks to take into account.

The disadvantages are just as persuasive as the advantages. Again, it all depends on your particular circumstances.

Let's have a look at some of the disadvantages of being classified as a share trader:

National Insurance

As your profits are treated as trading income, they are subject to national insurance, just as the profits from any other sole trader business. By contrast gains from share investments are not subject to national insurance.

A self employed share trader would be required to pay the following national insurance contributions:

- **Class 2** contributions - these are fixed at £2.10 per week for the 2005/2006 tax year. Annual bill: £109.20.
- **Class 4** contributions - 8% on profits between the lower and upper profit limits and 1% on profits above the upper profit limit.

For tax year 2005/2006, the lower earning limit is £4,895 and the upper earning limit is £32,760.

The Class 2 contributions are not very onerous but the Class 4 contributions essentially amount to an extra 8% to 9% tax charge, resulting in an overall tax rate of almost 50% for higher-rate taxpayers.

Example

John makes profits of £60,000 per year from his share trading activities. His national insurance is calculated as follows:

£32,760 - £4,895 @ 8%	*£2,229.20*
£60,000 - £32,760 @ 1%	*£272.40*
Class 4 national Insurance	*£2,501.60*
Class 2 national insurance	*£109.20*
Total national insurance	***£2,610.80***

SHARE TRADER – NATIONAL INSURANCE

Profits £	National Insurance £
10,000	518
20,000	1,318
30,000	2,118
40,000	2,411
50,000	2,511
60,000	2,611
70,000	2,711
80,000	2,811
90,000	2,911
100,000	3,011
130,000	3,311
150,000	3,511
180,000	3,811
200,000	4,011

The table above shows the total national insurance bill for different levels of profit during the 2005/2006 tax year. You'll see how the national insurance bill increases quite rapidly up to profits of £30,000, then the increases level off as the 8% rate is replaced by the additional 1% rate.

Whether this national insurance bill is worth paying depends on whether the benefits of share trader status, outlined above, more than cover this cost. We'll look at some overall calculations later.

Loss of Capital Gains Tax Reliefs

This is one of the most important factors weighing against share trader treatment.

For small investors and long-term investors the loss of capital gains tax reliefs, in particular the annual CGT exemption and taper relief, would probably prove disastrous from a tax-planning angle.

Small and long-term investors are unlikely to obtain trader treatment in the first instance. However, even the more wealthy trader could suffer from losing capital gains tax reliefs, in particular the annual exemption.

Unlike capital gains tax, income tax offers only one 'automatic' relief: the personal allowance. This allowance is far smaller than the annual capital gains tax allowance and would already be fully utilized if the share trader had other income.

As a rule of thumb, if the expenses you can now claim as a share trader do not exceed your annual capital gains tax allowance you will be no better off than when you were classified as an investor.

In fact, your expenses would have to more than exceed the capital gains tax allowance to also take account of your new national insurance bill.

The annual exemption is £8,500 in the case of one individual but £17,000 in the case of a married couple who own shares jointly. So the share trader would have to incur tax-deductible expenditure of more than £8,500 or maybe £17,000 before any tax savings are made from share trader status... and that doesn't even take national insurance into account.

If the individual has no other sources of income then the benefit of the personal allowance must also be brought into the calculation. In this case, your tax-deductible expenses must only exceed £3,605 (£8,500 - £4,895) before any benefit is gained. Once again this ignores national insurance.

So share trader status has its benefits (mainly tax-deductible expenses) but also drawbacks (loss of CGT reliefs and national insurance).

Tax Payments

Share traders, just like other sole traders, have to make income tax payments *during* the tax year and shortly after the end of the tax year.

With share investors it's completely different. Capital gains tax is only due to be paid by January 31 of the *following* tax year. This therefore gives share investors a valuable cash flow advantage as they can hold on to the taxman's money for up to 12 months longer.

Residency Issues

If you're planning to move overseas and become non-resident, being classed as a UK share trader would be disastrous.

An individual who becomes non-resident and non-UK ordinarily resident is exempt from UK capital gains tax on UK or overseas assets. This means that a share investor could become non-resident/ordinarily resident and sell UK shares with no UK taxes to pay. If the investor chooses an overseas country that doesn't have a capital gains tax, tax will be avoided altogether.

By contrast individuals who trade in the UK are still taxed on their profits even if they are non-resident. They could also be taxed in the overseas jurisdiction as well (although relief would be available to prevent a double tax charge). Therefore a non-resident share investor has significant advantages over a non-resident share trader.

Trading vs Investment: Numerical Examples

So how much do you stand to gain or lose by being classed as a share trader? The table on the next page shows the total tax payable by traders and investors at different profit levels.

TRADING VS INVESTMENT

Total Tax Bills Compared

(Assuming no tax-deductible expenditure)

Profits	1 Investor	2 Investors	Sole Trader	Partnership
£	£	£	£	£
10,000	150	0	1,390	256
20,000	2,091	300	4,390	2,780
30,000	4,091	2,182	7,390	5,780
40,000	6,091	4,182	10,370	8,780
50,000	9,911	6,182	14,470	11,780
60,000	13,911	8,182	18,570	14,780
70,000	17,911	10,182	22,670	17,466
80,000	21,911	12,182	26,770	20,740
90,000	25,911	15,822	30,870	24,840
100,000	29,911	19,822	34,970	28,940
110,000	33,911	23,822	39,070	33,040
120,000	37,911	27,822	43,170	37,140
130,000	41,911	31,822	47,270	41,240
140,000	45,911	35,822	51,370	45,340
150,000	49,911	39,822	55,470	49,440

There are two columns for investors (one for a single investor, the other for a married couple) and two columns for traders (one for a sole trader, the other for a married couple in partnership).

These tables are based on the taxpayers having no other taxable income. It's also important to note that the table assumes that the traders have no deductible expenditure (we incorporate that in the next example).

The message from the table is clear: there is no tax benefit to be derived from share trader status if you have little or no deductible expenditure. The share investor comes out on tops thanks to the annual CGT exemption and the fact that no national insurance is payable.

But what if there are significant costs, such as software, rent and subscriptions? Does this make trader classification more appealing?

An individual earning profits of £100,000 would pay capital gains tax of £29,911, or income tax and national insurance of £34,970. Therefore, in order to make share trader treatment worthwhile from a tax perspective, tax savings of over £5,059 would need to be achieved.

Let's now assume a share trader has a profit margin of 80% - in other words he makes £100,000 buying and selling shares and incurs expenses of £20,000. How would this impact on the final tax bill?

His tax as a sole trader would be:

	£
Profits (£100,000 x 80%)	80,000
Personal allowance	-4,895
Taxable income	75,105

Income tax:

£2,090 @ 10%	209
£30,310 @ 22%	6,668
£42,705 @ 40%	17,082
Total income tax	23,959
National insurance	2,811

Total income tax and national insurance £26,770

Now we start to see the possible advantages of trading status. A share *investor* with profits of £100,000 would pay tax of £29,911 because he cannot deduct many of his costs. In this example the trader enjoys a saving of more than £3,000 over the share investor.

TRADING VS INVESTMENT

Total Tax Bills Compared

(Trader's deductible expenditure amounts 10% or 20% of trading income)

Profits	Sole Trader Tax 10%	Sole Trader Tax 20%	Investor
£	£	£	£
10,000	1,090	790	150
20,000	3,790	3,190	2,091
30,000	6,490	5,590	4,091
40,000	8,730	7,090	6,091
50,000	12,420	10,370	9,911
60,000	16,110	13,650	13,911
70,000	19,800	16,930	17,911
80,000	23,490	20,210	21,911
90,000	27,180	23,490	25,911
100,000	30,870	26,770	29,911
110,000	34,560	30,050	33,911
120,000	38,250	33,330	37,911
130,000	41,940	36,610	41,911
140,000	45,630	39,890	45,911
150,000	49,320	43,170	49,911

The table above shows the total income tax and national insurance payable by a sole trader assuming a 10% or 20% reduction in profits due to allowable expenses.

This is then compared with the tax position of an investor who has the same expenses but cannot claim a tax deduction. To keep matters simple we again assume that both have no other taxable income during the 2005/2006 tax year.

The share trader still pays more tax than the investor on profits of £50,000 or less. After that there are tax savings to be had... but you have to be earning big profits and incurring a fair amount of tax-deductible expenditure.

The rest are better classed as share investors - and the good news is the taxman is likely to classify them as such!

In summary:

- If your profits do not exceed the annual CGT exemption (£8,500 or £17,000 for 2005/2006), it will always be beneficial to be classed as a share investor.
- If you make significant profits you could benefit by being classed as a share trader BUT you must have significantly high tax-deductible expenditure.
- If your profits are less than £50,000, it's very unlikely you will derive any benefit by being classed as a trader unless your expenses are abnormally high.
- If you are planning to emigrate, and continue your share dealing activities from overseas you need to be aware of the added tax disadvantages of trader status.

Remember there is no box to tick on your tax return to obtain share trader treatment — it's up to you to self assess your tax liability and complete your return on the basis of trading treatment if you feel this applies.

However, there are carefully defined rules as to when an individual will be regarded as trading as opposed to investing.

By having large trading capital, generating profits in excess of, say, £100,000 per year and running a professional business (perhaps running an office, too) would allow tax savings to be achieved and also convince the Inland Revenue that you are running a proper trading operation.

Chapter 24

Setting Up a Company to Save Tax

Serious share traders and investors often ask whether they should set up a company and whether this will produce attractive tax savings. In this chapter we'll take a detailed look at all the pros and cons.

Even after the 2004 Budget, which made some changes to the tax treatment of small companies, many ordinary businesses are still far better off incorporating. In recent years using a company has also been a popular tax-avoidance route for property investors. The idea is that, because corporation tax rates are generally very low, a company investor will earn far higher after-tax returns, which can be used to invest in new properties.

In this chapter we'll examine whether share investors and traders can follow a similar route. One of the main obstacles for share *investors* is the so-called Close Investment Company (CIC) provisions – these could make using a share *investment* company a costly alternative to direct ownership. Share *traders*, on the other hand, could potentially enjoy tax savings by setting up a company.

Offshore tax planning is also increasingly of interest to those with significant income and assets. Those wanting to escape the UK taxman often ask whether they can set up an offshore company located in a tax haven. It's possible but difficult - again we'll look at how and in what circumstances this could be achieved.

How Would a Company Work?

If you deal in shares as an individual, the profits are fully taxed in your hands, even if they are reinvested. Company profits are also fully taxed. However, there is no personal tax to pay by the company owner unless cash is actually extracted, either as a salary or a dividend. The advantage is that, although tax is payable on the company profits, corporation tax rates are generally much lower than personal tax rates, leaving the company with more funds to reinvest.

How the company is taxed will be influenced by whether the buying and selling amounts to share trading or share investing. This is the crucial factor.

Corporation Tax Rates

Company tax rates are generally much lower than income tax rates. Current corporation tax rates can be simply summarised as follows:

Tax Payable By Companies

On the first £10,000 profits	0%
On profits between £10,000 and £50,000	23.75%
On profits between £50,000 and £300,000	19%
On profits between £300,000 and £1.5m	32.75%
On profits over £1.5 m	30%

So, for example, a company with profits of £40,000 will pay 0% on the first £10,000 and 23,75% on the remaining £30,000. The total corporation tax bill will be £7,125.

A company with profits of £60,000 would pay 0% on the first £10,000, 23.75% on the next £40,000 and then 19% on the final £10,000. The total corporation tax bill would be £11,400.

Note that £11,400 is simply 19% of £60,000. So to make matters even more simple, it's worth remembering that once profits go over the £50,000 mark, the first two rates can be ignored and profits up to £300,000 are taxed at just 19%.

If your profits are £350,000 you will pay 19% tax on the first £300,000 and 32.75% on the extra £50,000.

Once profits exceed £1.5 million the calculation is also simple - all profits are taxed at a single rate of 30%.

Changes in the 2004 Budget

However, this is not the end of the matter. In the March 2004 Budget the Chancellor, Gordon Brown, felt that the use of the £10,000 tax-free band was being exploited and he changed the rate of corporation tax payable when a company *distributes* its profits as dividends, rather than reinvesting them.

The new provisions will ensure that when a company distributes profits to shareholders, those profits will be subject to corporation tax at a minimum rate of 19%.

Why Use a Company?

Many businesses (both trading and non-trading) use a company structure to reduce their tax bills by retaining cash within the company to reinvest and grow.

Keeping to this strategy allows only corporation tax to be paid on the profits (and remember corporation tax is much lower than income tax). Income tax would only be payable if cash was extracted by the owner.

However, when it comes to share *investment* companies, there is one key issue that could prevent the low tax rates from being exploited.

The Obstacle: Close Investment Companies

Investment companies are subject to different rules from trading companies. Many of the reliefs available to trading companies, such as business asset taper relief, rollover relief, and business property relief are NOT extended to investment companies.

As well as these specific provisions, there are also the Close Investment Company (CIC) provisions which apply to investment companies that are also 'close companies'.

The result of being classed as a CIC is that the lower rates of corporation tax are not available. Instead the company must pay tax at the 30% rate, irrespective of the level of profits.

Therefore, it's very important that we know exactly what a CIC is and when a company will fall within the definition.

What is a Close Investment Company (CIC)?

First of all we must explain what a 'close company' is. In practice almost all small owner-managed companies are 'close companies'. A close company is, generally speaking, any company that is controlled by:

- Its directors (including connected persons).
- Five or fewer participators. 'Participators' are generally shareholders, although this is a potentially wide term and can include loan creditors for a non-commercial loan.

Most companies are controlled by their directors and have fewer than five shareholders.

It's not a problem for a trading company to be classified as a close company. However, close companies that are also *investment* companies are specifically targeted. Just to make matters more confusing, the tax legislation defines a CIC in the negative. A company will be a close investment company *unless* it exists for one or more of the following purposes:

- Carrying on a trade or trades on a commercial basis.
- Making investments in land for letting to unconnected persons.

- Acting as a holding company, in other words holding shares in companies within a trading/property investment group.
- Co-ordinating the administration of two or more group companies involved in trading/property investment activities.

You'll notice that there is a let out for property investment companies... but there is no mercy for share investment companies. It is therefore likely that unless a company dealing in shares can be classed as a *share trading* company, it will be a CIC and pay tax at 30%.

Other Tax Consequences of Using a Company

One of the most important tax consequences of using a company is the loss of the annual capital gains tax allowance – £8,500 in the case of unmarried individuals and £17,000 if you're married and use a joint-dealing account.

For the very small share investor the loss of this exemption rules out using a company to buy and sell shares - no matter what advantages a company may offer, loss of the annual CGT allowance makes the whole exercise a waste of time.

The second point to note is the extra administrative burden of running a company. The rules governing the preparation of company accounts are stringent so you'll need to employ the services of an accountant - this all eats away at the tax savings you would otherwise have enjoyed.

Thirdly, taper relief does not apply to companies. Instead companies can claim Indexation Relief. This can be a major drawback, particularly for long-term investors or those that invest in shares that enjoy the higher rates of business asset taper relief (BATR), such as AIM shares.

We now know that the odds are stacked against the use of a company for share *investment* activities due to:

- The CIC provisions
- The loss of the annual CGT exemption
- The loss of taper relief
- The extra admin burden placed on company owners

As a general rule, share *investment* activities are taxed most favourably when the shares are held personally rather than through a company. It's the CIC provisions that do the real damage, resulting in a massive 30% tax charge before the profits are even extracted.

Summary

A company will generally NOT be tax efficient in the following circumstances:

- Where the shares purchased qualify for business asset taper relief the company option will lead to significantly higher tax charges. Shares that qualify for BATR include unquoted and AIM shares that are held for at least 12 months.
- Where any gains arising are relatively small and would be covered by the annual exemption (or two annual exemptions if the shareholder is married). Use of a company here would lead to a 30% tax charge.
- Where the shareholder needs all the proceeds to be extracted from the company. This leads to a double tax charge (corporation tax on the profits and income tax on the dividends).
- Where the taxpayer is a basic rate taxpayer and will pay capital gains tax at 20% on any gains realised. Here the rate of tax payable by the company under the Close Investment Company provisions exceeds the basic rate of tax payable by an individual.

On the other hand, a company could be tax efficient in the following circumstances:

- Where the company is not a CIC. We know that a share trading company would not be regarded as a CIC but in most circumstances a share investment company would fall within the provisions. One option is to use an exising company - see below.
- If the share gains are large and either substantial reinvestment of profits is anticipated or dividends are used to make use of the basic-rate tax band. This then optimises the two key advantages of corporate ownership, namely the tax-free nature of dividends for basic-rate taxpayers and the ability to reinvest profits.

Using an Existing Trading Company

You may already own your own trading company and carry on your share investment activities as a sideline.

One option in these circumstances would be to use your existing company to carry out your share dealing. The CIC provisions would only apply if the company exists 'wholly or mainly' for share investment activities during the accounting period.

If the share purchases are relatively small compared with other company assets and income, you could argue that the company is still a trading company and the CIC provisions therefore do not apply.

Note, you would need to carefully consider this to ensure that the company was not reclassified as an investment company. This would be disastrous and could prove costly in tax terms, particularly if the company was sold at a later date.

For taper relief purposes, the Inland Revenue will deny you business asset taper relief if more than 20% of the company's income or assets are attributable to non-trading activities - you'll therefore need to be careful about the extent of any share investment activities based on the level of the company's income and assets.

Pros and Cons of Offshore Companies

Investors often ask whether they can set up an offshore company (ie, non-UK resident company) to hold assets such as property or shares. What are the tax implications of this?

The first issue is to ascertain whether the company is truly a UK resident or offshore company.

A company is regarded as UK resident if it is either:

- A UK incorporated company, or
- Its central management and control is in the UK.

Central Management and Control (CM&C)

The Inland Revenue has stated that it will look at offshore companies to identify if there has been an attempt to create the *appearance* of central management and control, without it actually being exercised in the overseas location.

One common piece of advice is to use overseas directors to control the company. This can be accepted by Inland Revenue, however it would need to be looked at on a practical level.

Various cases have indicated that if the board of directors meet and give proper consideration to any transactions the company undertakes, such will constitute the central management and control. Inland Revenue may argue that the company is run by the controlling shareholder in the UK. If the overseas directors were simply puppets rubber stamping the UK resident shareholders' decisions, the company would be classed as UK resident.

Therefore, care is needed to ensure that any overseas directors are actually running the company.

In order to pass the CM&C test the majority of the directors should be non-UK resident and the non-UK resident directors should actively participate in making board decisions.

This means that key business decisions should be taken at overseas board meetings. A UK-resident shareholder may therefore establish a non-resident company but the running of the business has to be left to the non-resident directors

How Are Non-Resident Companies Taxed?

A UK-resident company is subject to UK corporation tax on its *worldwide* income and gains. By contrast a non-UK resident company is only subject to corporation tax on its *UK income* and is exempt from tax on gains from assets sold in the UK or overseas.

These rules are modified for companies that carry on a trade in the UK via a 'branch' or 'agency'. In these circumstances, gains from the sale of assets used in the UK trade are still subject to UK corporation tax.

If the offshore company is regarded as a share investor, any gains realised will be free of UK corporation tax, subject to the Inland Revenue tax anti-avoidance provisions discussed below.

Note that if the offshore company is regarded as a share trading company the shares would not be regarded as 'assets' but rather as trading stock. The impact of this would be that any profit on disposal would be treated as income, as opposed to a chargeable gain and, as such, subject to UK corporation tax.

Apportionment of Gains

This, however, is not the end of the matter. The Inland Revenue has targeted anti-avoidance legislation to reduce the opportunities for UK residents to use offshore companies to shelter gains.

These anti-avoidance provisions require the gains of a non-resident 'close' company to be apportioned amongst the member shareholders. CGT is levied on those who are resident and, in the case of individuals, domiciled in the UK.

We've already looked at what a close company is, and you'll remember that they include most owner-managed businesses.

Therefore a company incorporated overseas, and accepted by the Inland Revenue as being non-UK resident, could still have its gains taxed in the UK as a result of these provisions.

There are some significant exceptions to these provisions, such as where the UK-resident shareholders owns less than 10% of the share capital. In this case gains of the offshore company are not attributed to the UK-resident shareholder.

Non-resident Shareholders – Dividends

It is possible for an individual to retain cash within the company, then arrange for a dividend to be paid on becoming non-resident. The income tax rules regarding non-residence are more relaxed than the CGT rules. The non-resident shareholder could avoid liability to UK tax on the dividend by ensuring that he is non-resident throughout the relevant tax year of the dividend payment.

A non-resident can receive UK dividends tax free. There is no higher rate liability, and the notional tax credit is regarded as satisfying any basic rate tax liability.

Of course, care must be taken to ensure that the domestic tax legislation of your new country of residence, along with any double tax agreements, do not result in you 'jumping out of the frying pan and into the fire'.

Disposal of Shares in a Personal Company

What about the disposal of shares in the investment company itself?

The disposal of assets, whether UK or overseas, is outside the scope of UK CGT if an individual is non-UK resident, provided that the period of non-residence covers five complete and consecutive tax years and the asset is not used in a UK trading branch/agency.

Example

Phil has been using his personal company, Phil Ltd, to buy and sell shares for investment purposes.

He was non-resident from tax year 2002/2003 and decided to dispose of his shares in Phil Ltd during the 2003/2004 tax year.

As he is non-resident during the tax year the disposal takes place, no tax will be payable, provided Phil remains non-UK resident until 6 April 2008.

If Phil were to become UK resident during the 2005/2006 tax year, the gain would be subject to tax in that year.

Note that this treatment only applies to assets held at the date of departure from the UK. Therefore if Phil had acquired further UK shares directly whilst non-resident, these would not be subject to the five-year rule. Provided he was non-resident during the tax year of disposal, these later acquisitions would be exempt from UK CGT.

Non-residence is simply one of the circumstances in which a share investment company can be beneficial. In particular, the extraction of cash as dividends can be a useful mechanism to avoid the onerous CGT provisions. In practical terms it is therefore the shareholder's residence that can offer significant tax-planning opportunities.

Share Trading vs Investment Companies

In Chapter 23 we looked at the pros and cons of being classed as a share trader rather than a share investor. We showed that it is possible to benefit from income tax treatment rather than capital gains tax treatment... but only in a limited number of circumstances.

In this chapter we have already shown that there is very little benefit to be obtained from setting up a share *investment* company. The CIC provisions will subject the company to the 30% rate of corporation tax irrespective of its profit level, with further income tax payable when profits are extracted.

How about share *trading* companies? Remember, the CIC provisions apply to all close companies except (broadly) those carrying on a trade. Therefore, provided the Inland Revenue accepts that you are a share trader (see Chapter 23 for more information on how to be classed as a share trader), the CIC provisions will NOT apply and the company's profits will be taxed at much lower rates.

Tax Benefits of Share Trading Companies

The 19% corporation tax rate outlined earlier applies to profits of up to £300,000. For a sole trader, however, profits above £37,295 would be taxed at 40%. With corporation tax rates only half as high as income tax rates, it's easy to see why companies offer potentially attractive tax savings when profits are reinvested, preferably for many years.

If you want to pay out some of the profits you have a lot of flexibility because you can pay yourself the most tax-efficient mix of salary and dividends. Salaries and dividends are taxed in entirely different ways:

- Salaries are taxed at normal income tax rates (10%,22% or 40%). Dividends are taxed at 0% or an effective 25%.
- Salaries are subject to national insurance (above the lower earnings limit), dividends are not.
- Salaries are tax deductible for the company, dividends are not.

Which option is best will depend on how much other income you earn and the level of the company's profits. However, one route followed by many small business owners is to extract a small tax-free salary, equivalent to the annual personal allowance, and the remainder as dividends (tax free if you're a basic-rate taxpayer with no national insurance liability).

So how much tax do you stand to save if you operate a share trading company? The table on the next page compares the tax bills at different profit levels of the four categories of investor/trader we've analyzed in this guide. The first column is a share investor who pays capital gains tax on all his profits. The second is a sole trader who pays income tax on all his profits. The third is a share investment company (subject to the CIC provisions and taxed at 30%). Finally column four is the share trading company.

For the companies we've assumed all profits are extracted each year, with a small salary being taken to use up the company owner's personal allowance, with the rest taken as dividends. The tax bills for the two company columns are total tax bills taking into account the company's tax and the owner's personal tax.

TRADING VS INVESTMENT
COMPANY VS PERSONAL
Total Tax Bills Compared (£)

Profits	Investor	Trader	CIC Co	Trading Co
10,000	150	1,390	1,531	815
20,000	2,091	4,390	4,531	2,412
30,000	4,091	7,390	7,531	4,008
40,000	6,091	10,370	10,531	5,690
50,000	9,911	14,470	14,135	9,387
60,000	13,911	18,570	18,885	14,339
70,000	17,911	22,670	23,635	18,263
80,000	21,911	26,770	28,385	22,189
90,000	25,911	30,870	33,135	26,114
100,000	29,911	34,970	37,885	30,039
110,000	33,911	39,070	42,635	33,964
120,000	37,911	43,170	47,385	37,889
130,000	41,911	47,270	52,135	41,814
140,000	45,911	51,370	56,885	45,739
150,000	49,911	55,470	61,635	49,664

NOTES:
Investor – Owns shares personally, pays CGT
Trader – Owns shares personally, pays income tax
CIC Co – Company owns shares, pays tax at 30%
Trading Co – Company owns shares, pays tax at normal corporation tax rates

Up to now, being classified as a share investor (column one) has generally been much more attractive than being taxed as a trader (column two). However, if you use a share trading company (column four) and extract all the profits, the tax bills are very similar.

However, in the table we have overstated the tax bill of the share trading company because we have not included any tax-deductible expenditure in the calculation.

Remember the private investor cannot deduct any meaningful expenses whereas the share trading company can.

It's easy to see how this will generate further tax savings for the company route. For example, if the share trading company has income of £50,000 but expenses of £10,000, its taxable profits will be £40,000 and the total tax bill will be £5,690 rather than £10,370.

This is clearly much lower than the share investor's tax bill of £9,991!

The problem, of course, is you may have to convince the Inland Revenue that you are a share trading company rather than an investment company.

That's why we included column three as a reminder of the potential tax danger. In the above table the CIC company has the highest tax bill of all.

So you could end up with either the highest or the lowest possible tax bill, depending on whether the taxman classifies your company as a trader or an investor!

We've also ignored the fact that more than one person, eg a spouse, may be involved.

If you have a company with two shareholders this would result in even more tax savings due to the availability of two personal allowances and two basic-rate tax bands for dividend payments.

There are also capital gains tax benefits to be enjoyed by investors who own shares jointly with their spouses.

The table on the next page is similar to the table above, except in each case two persons are involved instead of one.

TRADING VS INVESTMENT COMPANY VS PERSONAL

Total Tax Bills Compared (£) – 2 Persons

Profits	2 Investors	Partnership	CIC Co	Trading Co
10,000	0	256	63	34
20,000	300	2,780	3063	1,630
30,000	2,182	5,780	6,063	3,227
40,000	4,182	8,780	9,063	4,823
50,000	6,182	11,780	12,063	6,420
60,000	8,182	14,780	15,063	9,540
70,000	10,182	17,466	18,063	11,440
80,000	12,182	20,740	21,063	13,340
90,000	15,822	24,840	24,063	16,902
100,000	19,822	28,940	28,270	20,827
110,000	23,822	33,040	33,020	24,752
120,000	27,822	37,140	37,770	28,677
130,000	31,822	41,240	42,520	32,602
140,000	35,822	45,340	47,270	36,527
150,000	39,822	49,440	57,020	40,452

NOTES:

Investor – Owns shares personally, pays CGT

Trader – Owns shares personally, pays income tax

CIC Co – Company owns shares, pays tax at 30%

Trading Co – Company owns shares, pays tax at normal corporation tax rates

Being classed as share investors (in other words, being entitled to two annual CGT exemptions) produces the best tax outcome at every profit level. However, this ignores costs. If there are, say, £10,000 of costs the company route is again more attractive.

COMPANY VS PERSONAL

Tax Bills Compared (£) – 50% Profits Reinvested

Profits	1 Investor	2 Investors	1 Person Co	2 Person Co
10,000	150	0	950	0
20,000	2,091	300	2,310	1,902
30,000	4,091	2,182	4,294	3,484
40,000	6,091	4,182	6,365	5,431
50,000	9,911	6,182	8,466	7,471
60,000	13,911	8,182	10,680	9,540
70,000	17,911	10,182	13,830	11,440
80,000	21,911	12,182	16,980	13,340
90,000	25,911	15,822	20,130	15,240
100,000	29,911	19,822	23,280	17,140
110,000	33,911	23,822	26,430	19,040
120,000	37,911	27,822	29,580	20,940
130,000	41,911	31,822	32,730	22,840
140,000	45,911	35,822	35,880	24,740
150,000	49,911	39,822	39,030	27,628

NOTES:
Investors – Owns shares personally, pays CGT
Company – Company owns shares, pays tax at normal corporation tax rates.

So far we've assumed all the profits are extracted from the company. However, one of the main reasons for setting up a company is so that profits can be reinvested without any personal tax being paid, just the low rates of corporation tax.

The table above shows the total tax payable by a one- and two-person company with the shareholders extracting 50% of the gross profits by way of a dividend after the payment of a salary equal to the personal allowance. The remaining 50% is retained within the company to pay corporation tax and reinvest in new share trades.

This is the best tax outcome possible. At certain profits levels the tax bill falls 30% when a company is used. The company owners can use these additional funds to make new share acquisitions.

What's more, we've excluded deductible expenditure which will reduce the company's tax bill even further, as shown above.

It's important to note that this is based on particular conditions such as no taper relief being claimed, no other income, and the annual exemption being available in full.

In real life, matters are not as straightforward as this, and there are occasions when corporate or individual ownership for both share trading and share investment would be the most beneficial option from a tax perspective.

Share Trading Company – Is it Possible?

The general rule is that it's easier for a company to be classed as a share trader than an individual.

All companies have articles of association and a memorandum of association. These are the internal rule books and are usually standard documents and for most companies, the shareholders will pay little attention to them.

However, it is possible to arrange for customised articles and a memorandum to be drawn up. It would strengthen your case for share trader classification to have these specially drafted.

In particular the memorandum of association often contains a number of paragraphs highlighting the objects of the company. These usually permit the company to carry out all activities of a 'general commercial company'. It would be helpful to show that the memorandum clearly shows the intention to be a share trader.

If there are other share investments contained within the company, the share trading activities would need to be substantial to class the company as a share trader and should be frequent and extend over as long a period as possible.

As with individuals, whether or not share transactions by a company amount to the carrying on of a trade is determined by the particular facts of the case in question, although it is less difficult for a company to be held to be a financial trader than an individual. Ultimately, if the taxpayer and the Inland Revenue cannot come to an agreement, it may be necessary to appeal to the Commissioners of the Inland Revenue to determine the matter.

It is impossible to simply set out 'rules' to be followed to obtain share trader status. These are covered in detail in Chapter 23 and they are all relevant to sole traders AND companies. In order to be classed as a trader, it would be expected that a trading activity should be organized in a professional manner. This ties in with all the other factors and is to a large extent the thread that underlies them all.

Take Peter, for example. Let's say he has a home office and spends five hours each day trading shares using a variety of sophisticated strategies. His portfolio is worth approximately £500,000 and this is his sole occupation.

In my opinion, Peter would have a strong case for being classed as a share trader - his activities have the appearance of a trade.

If Peter operated through a company, Peter's Trading Limited, in which he manages his own funds and those of other family members, it would be difficult to argue against the company being classed as a share trader. By showing a "deliberate and organized scheme of profit making" you are increasing the chances of share trading status being accepted.

Summary

As with all major decisions, there is no straightforward answer and the decision to engage in share dealing activities via a company would need to be carefully considered. Share investors are generally better off investing personally.

However, if you think your activities resemble a trade there is no reason why you could not take advantage of the benefits offered by incorporation, just as for any other business. You'd need to plough through the numbers to identify whether there would be any worthwhile tax savings taking into account the reinvestment levels, loss of reliefs, lower tax rates etc and then review whether you could actually persuade the Inland Revenue that you were actually a trading company. The worst case scenario would be for you to jump out of the frying pan and into the fire, and be classed as a share investment company being subject to the CIC provisions.

Appendix A

Tax Rates and Allowances

2003/2004 to 2005/2006

	Rates	**Bands, allowances, etc.**		
		2003/2004	2004/2005	2005/2006
		£	£	£
Income tax				
Personal allowance		4,615	4,745	4,895
Starting rate	10%	1,960	2,020	2,090
Basic rate	22%	28,540	29,380	30,310
Higher rate on over	40%	30,500	31,400	32,400
Pension earnings cap		99,000	102,000	105,600
Capital Gains Tax				
Annual exemption:				
Individuals		7,900	8,200	8,500
Trusts		3,950	4,100	4,250
Inheritance Tax				
Nil Rate Band Threshold		255,000	263,000	275,000
Pensioners, etc.				
Age allowance: 65 –74		6,610	6,830	7,090
Age allowance: 75 & over		6,720	6,950	7,220
MCA: born before 6/4/35		5,565	5,725	5,905
MCA: 75 & over		5,635	5,795	5,975
MCA minimum		2,150	2,210	2,280
Income limit		18,300	18,900	19,500
Blind Person's Allowance		1,510	1,560	1,610

Appendix B

Indexation Relief Rates

PERCENTAGES APPLYING TO DISPOSALS MADE AFTER APRIL 5 1998

Month of Acquisition	Rate %	Month of Acquisition	Rate %
March 1982 or earlier	104.7	July 1985	70.7
April 1982	100.6	August 1985	70.3
May 1982	99.2	September 1985	70.4
June 1982	98.7	October 1985	70.1
July 1982	98.6	November 1985	69.5
August 1982	98.5	December 1985	69.3
September 1982	98.7	January 1986	68.9
October 1982	97.7	February 1986	68.3
November 1982	96.7	March 1986	68.1
December 1982	97.1	April 1986	66.5
January 1983	96.8	May 1986	66.2
February 1983	96.0	June 1986	66.3
March 1983	95.6	July 1986	66.7
April 1983	92.9	August 1986	67.1
May 1983	92.1	September 1986	65.4
June 1983	91.7	October 1986	65.2
July 1983	90.6	November 1986	63.8
August 1983	89.8	December 1986	63.2
September 1983	88.9	January 1987	62.6
October 1983	88.3	February 1987	62.0
November 1983	87.6	March 1987	61.6
December 1983	87.1	April 1987	59.7
January 1984	87.2	May 1987	59.6
February 1984	86.5	June 1987	59.6
March 1984	85.9	July 1987	59.7
April 1984	83.4	August 1987	59.3
May 1984	82.8	September 1987	58.8
June 1984	82.3	October 1987	58.0
July 1984	82.5	November 1987	57.3
August 1984	80.8	December 1987	57.4
September 1984	80.4	January 1988	57.4
October 1984	79.3	February 1988	56.8
November 1984	78.8	March 1988	56.2
December 1984	78.9	April 1988	54.5
January 1985	78.3	May 1988	53.1
February 1985	76.9	June 1988	52.5
March 1985	75.2	July 1988	52.4
April 1985	71.6	August 1988	50.7
May 1985	70.8	September 1988	50.0
June 1985	70.4	October 1988	48.5

Appendix B (contd)

Month of Acquisition	Rate %	Month of Acquisition	Rate %
November 1988	47.8	September 1992	16.6
December 1988	47.4	October 1992	16.2
January 1989	46.5	November 1992	16.4
February 1989	45.4	December 1992	16.8
March 1989	44.8	January 1993	17.9
April 1989	42.3	February 1993	17.1
May 1989	41.4	March 1993	16.7
June 1989	40.9	April 1993	15.6
July 1989	40.8	May 1993	15.2
August 1989	40.4	June 1993	15.3
September 1989	39.5	July 1993	15.6
October 1989	38.4	August 1993	15.1
November 1989	37.2	September 1993	14.6
December 1989	36.9	October 1993	14.7
January 1990	36.1	November 1993	14.8
February 1990	35.3	December 1993	14.6
March 1990	33.9	January 1994	15.1
April 1990	30.0	February 1994	14.4
May 1990	28.8	March 1994	14.1
June 1990	28.3	April 1994	12.8
July 1990	28.2	May 1994	12.4
August 1990	26.9	June 1994	12.4
September 1990	25.8	July 1994	12.9
October 1990	24.8	August 1994	12.4
November 1990	25.1	September 1994	12.1
December 1990	25.2	October 1994	12.0
January 1991	24.9	November 1994	11.9
February 1991	24.2	December 1994	11.4
March 1991	23.7	January 1995	11.4
April 1991	22.2	February 1995	10.7
May 1991	21.8	March 1995	10.2
June 1991	21.3	April 1995	9.1
July 1991	21.5	May 1995	8.7
August 1991	21.3	June 1995	8.5
September 1991	20.8	July 1995	9.1
October 1991	20.4	August 1995	8.5
November 1991	19.9	September 1995	8.0
December 1991	19.8	October 1995	8.5
January 1992	19.9	November 1995	8.5
February 1992	19.3	December 1995	7.9
March 1992	18.9	January 1996	8.3
April 1992	17.1	February 1996	7.8
May 1992	16.7	March 1996	7.3
June 1992	16.7	April 1996	6.6
July 1992	17.1	May 1996	6.3
August 1992	17.1	June 1996	6.3

Appendix B (contd)

Month of Acquisition	Rate %
July 1996	6.7
August 1996	6.2
September 1996	5.7
October 1996	5.7
November 1996	5.7
December 1996	5.3
January 1997	5.3
February 1997	4.9
March 1997	4.6
April 1997	4.0
May 1997	3.6
June 1997	3.2
July 1997	3.2
August 1997	2.6
September 1997	2.1
October 1997	1.9
November 1997	1.9
December 1997	1.6
January 1998	1.9
February 1998	1.4
March 1998	1.1
April 1998 or later	0.0

TAX Cafe™

Pay Less Tax!

... with help from Taxcafe's unique tax guides and software

All available online at www.taxcafe.co.uk

- **How to Avoid Property Tax.** Essential reading for property investors who want to know all the tips and tricks to follow to pay less tax on their property profits.

- **Retire Rich with a Property Pension.** Everything you need to know about the new property pension rules, including how to buy property at a 40% discount, paid for by the taxman.

- **Non-Resident & Offshore Tax Planning.** How to exploit non-resident tax status to reduce your tax bill, plus advice on using offshore trusts and companies.

- **Using a Property Company to Save Tax.** How to massively increase your profits by using a property company... plus all the traps to avoid.

- **How to Avoid Inheritance Tax.** A-Z of inheritance tax planning, with clear explanations and numerous examples. Covers simple and sophisticated tax planning.

- **How to Avoid Stamp Duty.** Little known but perfectly legal trade secrets to reduce your stamp duty bill when buying or selling property.

- **ISAs – The Definitive Guide.** Find out how to invest in property tax free with an ISA plus dozens of other tips on maximizing your ISA tax savings.

- **Using a Company to Save Tax.** Everything you need to know about the tax benefits of using a company to run your business.

- **Bonus vs Dividend.** Shows how shareholder/directors of companies can save thousands in tax by choosing the optimal mix of bonus and dividend.

- **How to Avoid Tax on Your Stock Market Profits.** How to pay less capital gains tax, income tax and inheritance tax on your stock market investments and dealings.

- **Selling a Sole Trader Business.** A potential minefield with numerous traps to avoid but significant tax-saving opportunities.

- **How to Claim Tax Credits.** Even families with higher incomes can make successful tax credit claims. This guide shows how much you can claim and how to go about it.

- **Property Capital Gains Tax Calculator.** Unique software that performs complex capital gains tax calculations in seconds.

Printed in the United Kingdom
by Lightning Source UK Ltd.
108566UKS00002B/64-102